Warm Flat Beer

Arturo's
WARM FLAT
BEER

Art "Arturo" Belge

Shuleen
Hope you love it
Art "Arturo" Belge

ISBN: 978-1-938394-11-9

Library of Congress Control Number: 2014950170

Published by
Great Life Press
Rye, New Hampshire 03870
www.greatlifepress.com

Cover art, book, and website design by Grace Peirce

Additional copies available from:

Brian Belge
warmflatbeer.com
email: brian@warmflatbeer.com

Dedication

She was quite young, just a score and three,
When she pledged her love, and married me.
Our clan was large, with trials enough,
But she was made of stronger stuff.
Like the oak protects the farmer's field,
Her strength became our family shield.
For character, beauty, and a generous soul;
For trying to teach me self-control;
For all that she is, I thank my wife:
My Guiding Starr, my love and my life.

Thanks . . .

To Rick Fresina for the nudge; Debbie Driedger for her keen eye; Grace Peirce for her book smarts; my daughter, Sandy Labyris, for finishing my sentences; and my son, Brian Belge, for finishing my thoughts.

Intro to Art

Arthur J. Belge was born in the parlor of his parent's house in Syracuse, New York. That is undoubtedly why, psychologically speaking, he chose to make a living in a business that depended largely on home-delivery. But I get ahead of myself.

After graduating from college with a business degree, Art was able to employ his newfound business acumen on the General Electric television bulb assembly line. This mind-numbing experience made him particularly suited to teaching high school geography.

From there, the most obvious career choice he could make was selling pizza to the masses. Some of his friends and family didn't think it was a very good idea, but the rest were vehemently opposed, so he knew he was on to something.

And that is how he became a restaurateur.

And that is how this book came to be. You see, as a member of a respected community, he agreed to write a series of columns for a monthly publication dedicated to promoting the restaurant scene in and around Syracuse. His only caveat was that his articles didn't have to have anything to do with promoting the restaurant scene in and around Syracuse—which they didn't, as you will see.

When he first opened Arturo's Pizza Shop on James Street in Eastwood, Art had some solid views of what he wanted his pizza to be: Fresh dough, fresh vegetables, top quality mozzarella, and his own homemade sauce and sausage.

He rented a small space next to a barbershop, and, over the next four years, built a faithful clientèle. Once they tasted his pizza, he had them hooked.

Four years later, the restaurant on the corner of James and Woodbine came up for sale. Art, now known as "Arturo," which, of course, is Italian for Arthur, signed a lease and doubled his space. A while later, the storefront next to his became vacant and he better than doubled his seating space again and expanded the menu.

For the next twenty-eight years, Art worked on turning Arturo's into a camp place to be. He gave all the menu items double entendre names, and put humorous signs on the walls like: *"Please don't talk to our plants, they are spoiled already!"* and *"Please refrain from taking our 69 cent candle-holders, so we can afford more expensive ones for you to steal."*

Arturo's carafes and wine glasses were all labeled *Cheap Wine*. The draft beer pitchers and pints all had *Arturo's Warm Flat Beer* emblazoned on them—hence the title of this tome.

Several people advised Art that everyone may not appreciate his humor. He would usually respond with something like, "Hey, if I'm not gonna get filthy rich, I'm damn sure gonna have some dirty fun." One woman wrote a scathing letter taking him to task for his blatant taste in words and his earthy humor. He framed it and hung it on the wall.

Arturo's occupied the last two storefronts out of six, all with a single back hall running behind them. This configuration gave rise to the restaurant's one serious drawback: the only public restrooms in the whole building were at the opposite end of that hall. That's right, the restrooms were literally a city block away from the dining room. Customers—especially the beer drinkers—complained about the long trek.

Arturo turned the problem into an opportunity by hitting it head-on with humor. He had big, clip-on buttons made that read: *I Have Made the Long 'Hall' at ARTURO'S*. The staff would put one on a customer's placemat while they were "down the hall," as the crew euphemistically put it. Soon, these people were bringing new customers in just to see their faces when they got their buttons.

Outside the restaurant there hung an old Pepsi sign. Art painted it over with "Arturo's *DECENT* Italian Food." This understated promise did more to bring in new customers than anything else he ever did.

As the business expanded, it grew beyond the limitations

of its tiny kitchen and lack of parking, so, when Arturo found a restaurant in Mattydale that was up for sale, he bought it.

He now had a full scale, free-standing building under his personal control with a large dining room, a full service bar, and a large parking lot. Art continued to serve his signature dishes with healthy dollops of humor until 1994, when, after 35 years in business, he turned his pizza ovens off for the very last time.

Art Belge now lives with his wife in picture perfect Mazatlan, Mexico where they have become renowned for throwing 'not to be missed' rooftop dinner parties. However, a continuing testimonial to their legacy in Syracuse can be found in the Arturo's parties hosted by Tom and Denise Gillies where former staff, loyal customers, family, and friends all gather together to visit with Art and Starr on their annual sojourns to the Salt City. Everyone catches up on new news, reminisces about the salad days of old, laughs a lot, hugs a lot, and feasts like royalty. And what food do they serve their honored guests? Why, Arturo's Decent Italian Food, of course!

Contents

The Salt City Kid

1. The Great Corn Raid

A good trial lawyer must think quickly on his feet, and nobody did the Attorney Two-Step better than my eldest brother, Duke. That notwithstanding, I remember a time, long before he became one of Syracuse's most innovative lawyers, when Duke thought quickly *on his belly.*

It was when he and Luke, our middle brother, were both in their early teens. They decided to have a corn roast along with several of their buddies. The corn would be obtained in the traditional way, by raiding a neighbor's garden.

To my surprise they allowed me, their eight-year-old brother, to go with them on the raid. Well, of course, I did offer a persuasive argument, "Take me with you, or I'll squeal." Which they did not counter with their usual, "Do, and you'll get your face broken!"—a threat I accepted as having higher trump value than mine. Perhaps they were mellowing. In any event, I didn't question my luck—or them, knowing in my heart that they considered me a thorn in their sides.

I was disappointed I wouldn't be allowed to stay up late enough to go to the corn roast, but I was thrilled to be in on the raid. Besides, I could pick some tomatoes while the big guys were absconding the corn, and tomatoes are almost as prime eating as corn. Of course, nothing beats fresh corn on the cob, but fresh picked tomatoes come in a damn close second.

Do you remember roasting corn over a wood fire? The streaks of burnt kernels alternating with streaks of raw could not dissuade you from swearing that it was anything but the most delicious corn, ever. The same was true of potatoes baked in the wood coals. The skins turned black and bitter, but we convinced ourselves that was exactly what made them sooooo delicious.

That night, Duke boosted me over the fence that surrounded three sides of the backyard garden. Then he and his cohorts joined me by way of the nextdoor neighbor's garage extension. You see, after WWII, the newer cars had longer engines. To accommodate the longer engine compartments, a garage owner would cut out a four-foot-high section of the back wall and build a cubbyhole for the front of the car to tuck into—and for delinquent young rapscallions to jump from to get into the neighboring gardens.

The boys started harvesting the corn immediately, while I stole away and loaded up my tummy with plump, ripe tomatoes.

Suddenly, two policemen and the gardener, let's call him Farmer Brown, descended upon us. Duke hissed at me, "freeze!" and we froze. All of the other boys scattered, clambering over the fence, and headed for the hills. All except Stinky Wilson's older brother, who was literally flying by the seat of his pants, having been caught by the wires protruding from the top of the fence.

Duke grabbed me by the scruff and boosted me over, then climbed over himself. That made us the last ones out—and the only ones who saw Joey's predicament. Duke pushed me under some bushes, and, lying down flat beside me, peered back, assessing the situation.

It seems Farmer Brown and one of the policemen had run up the driveway to the street, hoping to catch any of the boys sneaking out of neighboring yards. The other policeman hauled Joey off the fence, and marched him from behind, booting him with his knee with each step. Duke put his hand on my back and whispered, "Don't move!" He rose without a sound, stealthily climbed the fence, sneaked up behind Joey and his captor...and booted the cop stoutly in the arse, hollering, "Catch *me*, flatfoot!" And then took off running.

Taken by surprise, the officer let go of Joey and took off after Duke. "Run, Joey, run!" my brother yelled over his shoulder. And run Joey did. Propelled by the fear of being caught by a kicked cop, he easily cleared the fence this time. Duke ran in the other direction, up the driveway, right past the startled Farmer Brown and the other policeman, who reacted too late to do anything but watch him disappear into the yards across the street.

The boys found each other a short while later, and spent hours reliving and congratulating themselves on their great escapade, and forgetting entirely about their corn. They had also forgotten about the little brother, who, scared out of his wits, stayed under the bushes right where he was told to until way after dark.

I eventually got brave enough to sneak home. I had not only missed supper, I had missed the far more serious be-home-before-the-street-lights-come-on curfew by over an hour. Not daring to tell the truth, I mumbled some half-baked lie and, after joining Joey and Joey's policeman in the exclusive no-thank-you-I'd-rather-stand-than-sit club, was sent to bed without supper.

But I didn't mind really. Had I told my mother the truth, my brother would've inducted me into a new club with far more clout: The Sibling Revenge Society. I'm pretty sure it would have had only two members: my big brother, Duke, and *me*. Besides, I'd been out on a Grown-Up Adventure and stuffed myself with Farmer Brown's juicy tomatoes.

I went to serve my sentence a very, very, happy lad, counting my blessings, sore bottom and all.

2. Stinky Wilson

Honestly, you really couldn't blame me.

I mean, how could I not laugh—what with Stinky running around the yard, waving his flaming hand, doing the best impression of the Olympic torch runner I'd ever seen? Well, sure, he wasn't doing it on purpose; it was just one of those things that an odd circumstance sometimes brings about.

Unfortunately, Stinky didn't have my ability to view the event from an objective perspective, so he didn't take it quite as philosophically as I thought he should. As I recall it now, he was actually a little miffed at me for laughing. I think he screamed something like, "Imgonnakillya!"

Hey! I'm not the one who spilled kerosene on my hand when I filled the blowtorch, and then went right ahead and lit the damn thing, anyway.

You see, back in the Depression years, most homes were heated with coal, but a few—like Stinky's—were heated with kerosene. Kerosene was cheap. It also stank.

And that's how Stinky got his malodorous moniker.

We had just had an accident with our soapbox derby, which is what we called an orange crate on a plank on two baby buggy axles on four wheels, no two alike. We hadn't quite caught on to the subtle difference between the race and the racecar, so the jalopies we built were called by the name of the race. Adults corrected us. But what did they know? By the sagacious age of ten, we had learned to ignore their irrelevant hair-splitting as we set off to do more important things like racing our own soapbox derbies in our own soapbox derbies.

On this particular day, our soapbox derby lost a cotter pin. Then it lost a wheel and, finally, it lost an argument with an elm tree that took as stubborn a stance as Nixon did on Watergate, which was more than the nation could bear on the one hand, and more than our axle could bear on the...*Look ma, no hands!*

"We could stick the axle in your coal furnace," Stinky said. "And when the metal turns red, it would be real simple to straighten it out."

I was proud of Stinky. This, for him, was a brilliant thought, because any thought that had both a noun and a verb was for Stinky a brilliant thought. The fact that it was thought up weeks after the breakdown did diminish it a bit, but it also put us on the right track: we needed heat. To avoid getting caught banging around in the cellar, we rooted out my father's blowtorch, instead. We took it out to the back lot, but alas and a lack of fuel put us back at square none.

Wait a minute, I thought to myself—and to no one else, since there was no one else in my head I could think to at the time—I have a brilliant idea of my own!

"Got any kerosene in your cellar, Stinky?"

"Could be."

"Find out."

He returned with a full can and proudly, albeit sloppily, filled the blowtorch. He then proceeded to light the torch...

...bringing us back to Stinky, the Human Torch.

Stinky learned the first two laws of the Two Laws of Combustibility that day: One. Never light a blowtorch before wiping the spillage off your hands. And two. Never light a blowtorch before wiping the spillage off your hands.

3. Stinky Gets Tanked, Again

Stinky Wilson wasn't blessed with both an older older-brother and a younger older-brother like I was; he only had the one older-brother, who, along with my younger older-brother and a couple of their buddies, who could have been each others' brothers for all I know, pitched in and bought a very-much-used used car. This is something kids today cannot experience. Back then, before there were mandatory auto inspections and compulsory insurance, you could put anything on the road if you bought it and you got a license. We used to say we held our clunkers together with spit and bailing wire. That's ridiculous, of course. We used chewing gum, pixie sticks and desperately mumbled prayers to Saint Johnpauljude.

Just to show you how things were back in those good old days: about six years after the time we're talking about, when I was in college, I allotted ten dollars a week in my budget for automotive expenses. This included gas, oil, insurance, which had become mandatory by then, and repairs. And I never paid more than $75 for a car to begin with. Probably because that's the most anyone would let me borrow. Any repair that would cost more than $40 was cause for the vehicle's consignment to the Fulton Scrap Metal Yard, because the scrap yard would pay that amount for it. By putting another $30 or so along with that $40, plus two bucks registration transfer fee, I had another vehicle on the road for less than the repair on my old car would have cost. Let's see you come anywhere near that today.

Back to everybody's brothers' jalopy.

It was in that car that I learned that a wheel that comes off a car that is in fast motion will pass that car in faster motion.

There are two things I would like to point out about that last statement. One, while it sounds like an impossibility—a part being greater than the whole of its something or other—it is, so help me Hannah, true. And, two, I used the word "that" six times.

By the way, I learned the interesting fact about wheels while we were on our way to Welch's Construction. Timing is everything.

I guess I'll have to stop for a second here and explain Welch's Construction to you. Welch's Construction is a quarry pit near Minoa that filled with water when a steam shovel hit the same underground stream that feeds Green Lakes. Or so a person told me. The pit was several hundred feet deep, and supposedly filled so rapidly that the shovel and several trucks were abandoned, never to be recovered. Or so a lot of people say. Why, someone's cousin's best friend knows a guy who actually swam down far enough to see them! So everyone says.

But this is another thing that today's youngsters will never experience firsthand, because the last I knew, troopers patrol the pit, and signs have been posted warning of deportation to jail—or worse yet, to Buffalo—for trespassers. Those several kids who went there to drown every year ruined it for everyone else. Several of us had planned to get scuba gear when we were grown up and had jobs, and make the underwater trek from Green Lakes to Welch's, but that's all ruined now, too, I guess.

What has this got to do with anything? Geez! Be patient willya? I'm getting to that.

One day the boys ran out of gas and gas money at the same time. Not an unusual circumstance, except this day they had the same brainstorm that I had several years earlier: Stinky's family's kerosene storage tank. Though much younger, I was always the more brilliant, touched on the shoulder at birth by the avant garde sword, so to speak. They put a couple of gallons of kerosene in the car, and by jingo, it worked! They drove around and had a grand old time, until they tried to shut it off. It burned so hot that the engine obeyed the key about as well as we kids did when our parents told us not to go near Welch's Construction.

The smell and billowing clouds of kerosene smoke attracted a crowd. With a life of its own, the engine continued to run.

Afraid that the overheating engine would blow up, they eventually stopped it by dousing it with buckets of cold water. I can't begin to describe the metallic, grinding, hissing, screeching, high pitched, banshee wailing sound, so I won't.

Thus we all learned the Third Law of Combustibility: Furnaces, blowtorches, and Stinky Wilson's hand may all run well on kerosene, but cars do not.

The Fulton Scrap Yard got a new heap of old junk that day. And for his similar efforts years before, Stinky Wilson got a gauze bandage, a good scolding, and a really nifty scar that all the girls oohed and aahed over, the lucky bastard.

4. Frenchy's Revolution

I became friends with Frenchy when we were in grammar school together at St. Vengeance de Paul on Burnet Ave. One day, Frenchy invented a game he called *When You See a Car Coming Up Teall Avenue Wait Until the Very Last Second Then Race in Front of the Car and Cross the Street as Fast as You Can.* If you didn't make it to the other side of the road, you were disqualified.

We played for hours. Eventually, Mrs. Frenchy—that is, Frenchy's mother, not his wife—noticed us through her living room window. Oblivious to the devilish nature of her own child, she naturally assumed such a harebrained idea had to be mine. She chased me off and dragged poor Frenchy home by his ear, loudly warning him that he was "never, ever going to play with that crazy Artie Belge again," so help her God!

Now, in those days, when parents spoke, children listened. Frenchy and I knew in our bones that an edict like that was to be taken as Gospel, so naturally, we became best friends. We even became blood brothers.

One fall Saturday, Frenchy and I skulked around the neighborhood, raiding all the front yards, pillaging horse chestnuts. We also found a few road apples along the way, which Frenchy judiciously applied to the broadside of Old Man Watzizheimer's tool shed.

When we got back, we sat on my back porch with our ill-gotten chestnuts, making necklaces and Indian armbands and "t'baccy" pipes out of them. We had around a bushel-and-a-half all told, but after using up just a fraction of them, we were wallowing in boredom.

Idly flinging chestnuts into the air, Frenchy stood up and sent one flying over the wholesale florist shop next door. Now, it just so happened that the flower shop consisted of six glass greenhouses standing in a row. Chestnut...glass greenhouse...the result was inevitable. Frenchy's chestnut, descending in a smooth arc over the first glass house, hit the second slanted glass roof with a loud *tink!*

Uh, oh.

And then...another tink! The chestnut had bounced back to the first roof!

It tinked from roof to roof and back again a few times, then rolled down into the alley between the two glass structures. I had to admit it, it was pretty neat. Still, I told him not to throw any more because my parents would tan my hide if we got caught. But he threw another before I could stop him, pointing out that the chestnuts weren't even breaking the windows—they were bouncing right off of them!

And by goshen, he was right! Not only that, but the higher he threw them, the more they volleyed back and forth between the slanted panes of glass.

The contest was on! We competed until we'd used up every last chestnut in the bushel. Then we broke up the necklaces and Indian arm bracelets and make-believe t'backy pipes, and played some more. What fun!

Later on, this being a Saturday and thus date night, my elder sister was primping in the bathroom. Our parents had gone out for the evening, so when there was a loud knock at the door, I opened it.

It was a cop.

"H-H-hello, off-officer," I stammered. "M-m-may I h-help you?"

He said he was inquiring about someone breaking 127 glass panes in the greenhouses next door by throwing chestnuts at them.

"W-w-well that w-w-wouldn't break them w-w-would it? They'd just b-b-bounce, wouldn't they?"

Something about my question must have tipped him off; I saw it in his eyes. And I knew he could see the terror in mine. I thought he was gonna kill me—but he didn't. I like to think it was more the uncontrollable knocking of my knees, and less the spontaneous release of my bladder, that moved him to pity—but, alas, I'll never know for sure.

"No, but they're all cracked and must be replaced," he said. "It's not something we'd want to see happen again, now, is it?"

"N-no, Sir!" I exclaimed, with exuberant civic passion.

Looking sternly into my eyes once more, he shook my hand, thanked me for my assistance, and quit the doorstep.

When my elder sister came out of the bathroom, she asked who was at the door.

I replied, "Jehovah's witnesses."

She said, "That doesn't seem right, they always come on Sunday."

"Yeh! They said something about their summer picnic being tomorrow."

A few years later, Frenchy and I found my father's cigarette rolling machine and some cigarette papers—relics of *The Depression*. If you were alive back then, you'll remember it was always said that way, *"The Depression,"* like there never had been such an unmitigated disaster before and there never could be anything like it, ever again. Like "The War to End All Wars." That was supposed to be it. Done. Fini. Kaput. But it was such a hit at the box office, they had to repackage it as "World War I" when they rolled out the sequel to start all sequels, WWII. Anyway, we started messing around with the rolling machine, figuring out how it worked. If we ever got some money we could buy some tobacco and roll some smokes and be the most daring lords of the schoolyard.

"Wait, I just got a great idea!" I effused. I grabbed the family pencil sharpener, put a cigarette paper in the roller and shook some of the pencil shavings into the roller. It was pure genius! Except for a few black spots from the lead shavings, it looked like a real cigarette. Once we learned to make sure the lead wasn't near the ends, we had a dozen perfect specimens.

We never even lit them up, never mind inhaling; remember, we were in it for the sophistication.

After a while, we headed over to Frenchy's house to score some Pepsi. Everybody drank Pepsi in those days because you got twelve ounces. A Coke bottle only held eight. Remember the jingle? *"Pepsi Cola hits the spot...twelve full ounces that's a lot!"*

When we got to Frenchy's house, we saw his dad standing on the porch. Frenchy quietly asked me for one of the mockarettes. I handed it over and he stuck it behind his ear.

Now, every kid thought that Mr. Frenchy—that is, Frenchy's father, not his husband—was a cool guy even before the term "cool" was cool. We all *knew* that when he was a young man he was a rum runner (whatever that was) during Prohibition (whenever that was). So, there he was, standing on the steps, arms crossed, muscles bulging, when his son walked across the porch and, without a word, walked stiffly past him.

His father grabbed him by the arm and swung him around to face him. "What's that in your ear, boy?"

"Oh, ah, er, that's just a pre-pre-pretend cigarette," he stammered, pretending to be nervous. "I was just going to show it to Mom."

"Yeh, right! That ain't no pretend cigarette. I oughta tan your britches! Give me that thing, boy!"

He snatched the mockarette from behind his son's ear, whipped out his Zippo lighter, and inhaled deeply.

He choked. He coughed. He sputtered.

His face turned redder than red. It looked as though his ears were going to shoot sparks. And the instant he stopped puffing, the mockarette burst into flames. He knew he'd been had. He shot out a hand, grabbing for his son, but Frenchy took off like he'd been goosed with a corn cob. Clearing the stairs in one giant leap, he was gone.

I wasn't far behind.

Frenchy was on my porch when I got home. He spent that night—and the next—and the next—at my house. He called his mom each day to see if his dad had cooled down enough so he could come home.

It took about a week.

Frenchy and I ended up going to different high schools, so we only saw each other occasionally.

On one such occasion, Frenchy joined a bunch of my friends in a dealer's choice poker game. Man! He was staying in and bidding on every hand. He was like a fly on Carmen Veranda's still-life-with-fruit-salad hat; you couldn't swat him away with a tennis racket.

I asked his friend, Cosmo, what Frenchy was doing.

"He's losing his ass."

"Well I can see that. But why is he staying in to the end of every hand?" I asked. "Is it a death-wish?"

"Close enough," whispered Coz. "He's the senior class treasurer and he blew their funds. Brother Cough Drops (the faculty moderator of the Order of No Remorse at Christ Was a Wimp High School) already hates him. He might put him in jail!"

Somehow, he escaped that fate, because I saw Frenchy and Cosmo again several months later. They were being escorted out of the Loews State Movie Theater. Seems they were caught sneaking in the side door. But that was no big deal; everybody did it.

I never saw Frenchy again, but I did see Coz several years later in a neighborhood vomitorium. A guy came in, went right to the bartender, and asked who owned the luxury car parked at the curb.

"Cosmo."

"Well there's a big ass drunk passed out on the hood and his belt buckle is scratching the bejesus out of the damn thing."

The bartender went to the window and looked out.

"I see what you mean."

"Think we should tell this Cosmo fellow?"

"Nope."

"Mind if I ask why?"

"That *is* Cosmo."

And that just goes to show you that "Crazy Artie" didn't turn out to be the craziest of Frenchy's pals, after all—not by a long shot. Anyone up for a quick game of *When You See a Car Coming Up Teall Avenue?*

5. Musically Impaired

At some stage in every child's life, they decide that they want to play a musical instrument. Some primal draw to the jungle drums, I guess. Or maybe it's just that kids get a lot of dumb ideas, and this is just another one of them.

I know a lot of the kids I grew up with had a lot of dumb, even Lukey, ideas, but fortunately for my parents, I wasn't one of those. Except for getting a bug to play the Western guitar this one time, I was pretty levelheaded.

Oh sure, there was the time I was going to dig an underground hut to end all underground huts. No open pit for me, with boards, rugs and tar-paper covering it. Oh no! When I say underground, I mean dig a hole in the earth, and then tunnel a colliery in from that. Nothing wacky about that. To bad for me though, the woman who lived next door to the lot where I was playing groundhog engineer suffered from dangeraphobia; consequently, she kept filling the mine shaft with ashes. I didn't get mad—I just dug them out and started clawing my way into the entrails of the earth again. The reason I didn't get mad was that deep in my heart I knew she was working from the best of motives.

And somewhere in my medulla obshortgata, I knew she was right. It still amazes me that three of the 174 things that I am afraid of are suffocation, the dark, and snakes. Yet there I was digging a pit and cave in the middle of an overgrown lot.

Let me ask you: do you look askance at holding a Soap Box Derby Race down the center of Wilson Street Hill, with the cotter pins removed so that the wheels could fall off? I mean, if you could keep those wheels on, while the rest of the guys were crashing into trees, curbs, and telephone poles—well if you don't understand it, I can never explain it.

And what was so wrong in using the railroad tracks to get to the swimming hole in the old, abandoned quarry? So what if trains still used those tracks—it wasn't often. Well, somebody said it wasn't. I mean, it saved a quarter of a mile walking, and if a train did come, I was pretty sure we could get off the trestle in time. Wasn't it worth a little risk to hasten getting to the swimming hole where there were no lifeguards, or *any* adults at all, to bug you?

The point I'm trying to get across is that brains that operate like that do not take mere facts into consideration. So it is with the taking up of a musical instrument. For instance, in my family, our singing voices sound like a cross between an abandoned basset hound and a water buffalo in heat. Also, none of us could read music, although our combination music and Latin teacher at school, Sister Puella-Cantata of the Order of the Declension of the Immaculate Verb, had been trying to teach us to do so for umpteen years. All our minds knew was that we wanted to play and sing like Roy Rogers, and perhaps push Pat Brady aside and drive his jeep, Nellie Belle, now and then. You younger readers, 99.14% of you, must understand that when I was nine, Roy Rogers was our answer to the Beatles, long before the Beatles were even a question.

No, this mind did not comprehend that you can't make a silk musician out of a tin ear.

Well, it didn't matter. As it turned out, any possibility of a future engagement playing my Western guitar in Carnegie Hall backed by the New York Philharmonic Orchestra was doomed from the start. It seems that one of my older siblings had been allowed to exercise a stupid yen to play the Hawaiian guitar. The Hawaiian guitar sits on your lap, not on your chest. You work a steel bar along the fret with one hand while you pluck the strings with the other.

How was that practical? I mean, nobody, just nobody, plays a Hawaiian guitar while riding a horse. You couldn't do it riding in the passenger seat of Nellie Belle, either, not without jabbing Pat in the ribs so many times that he'd have to stop the jeep to smash either you or the overgrown lap uke against a tree.

I didn't stand a chance. My Depression-scarred—and scared—parents just didn't waste things. There was "a perfectly good guitar in the house, and Western-schmestern, if you want to play an instrument, that's what you'll play." I don't blame them, now. The fact that I can't remember which brother or sister played it means that they most likely didn't play it long. So Mom could talk my once-burned Dad into springing for the lessons, but she wasn't going to get him to sponsor a two-instruments-in-the-attic family.

I played that thing for a little over a year. I did everything that a music student should do...except practice. At my first recital, I performed "Mary Had a Little Lamb"; at my second, it was "Merrily We Roll Along." No one in the audience seemed to notice the great progress I had made.

Shortly after that, I went for what was to be my last weekly lesson, and was soundly (pun intended) berated for not having practiced. "You will sit here, young man, while I go downstairs and do some housework," the teacher said, "and practice for an hour. Then I will come back up and give you a lesson."

Didn't she know the guys were playing softball? Apparently not, but I did. I opened the window, climbed out on the porch roof, slid down the post, and strode off into the sunset.

I didn't have any younger brothers, but if I did, they would undoubtedly be thanking me to this very day because I'm pretty sure that tinny old Hawaiian six-string is still sitting right there on the chair where I left it. What can I say? To a lad, the gentle strums of an old guitar were no match for the pounding drums of summer.

6. Artie at the Bat

'Twas the twilight of summer, the end of vacation;
Of the national game, we'd had too small a ration.
Day after day we played in the park
And batted at pitches 'til way after dark.

But time marched along, and summer passed by;
Before we kids knew it, the last game was nigh.
And then in a flash, we were in the last inning;
They had us by one, they were counting on winning!

It was my turn at bat. The coach told me, "Son,
Go for the single; forget the home run."
Still, a homer or triple would win the whole show;
If I were to hit it, I'd say "luck, doncha know!"

From the plate to the fence was about eighty yards,
And I knew in my heart it was not in the cards.
So I made up my mind not to go for the fence,
Hitting a single made oodles more sense.

But what do you do with a lob for a pitch?
Just haul off and wallop that sonofabitch!
The outfielder runs, he peers overhead,
He chugs like a freight train, closing the spread.

He climbs up the fence, he leans for the ball,
He teeters, he totters—maybe he'll fall—
He stretches his arm, the spectators roar,
He steals my home run, that son of a whore!

That loss should have taught me a lesson that day,
But the truth is I've never discovered a way
To soften my blows, to keep my mouth shut,
To follow my head instead of my gut;

I swing for the fences, I go for the score;
When I get what I want, I go after more.
Win, lose, or draw doesn't matter to me—
My tale at the bar gets me whiskey for free!

7. True Confession

The Guilt

There is no presumption of innocence; it's all about the guilt.

And nobody—with the exception of all mothers, every-where—knows how to inculcate guilt better than the Catholic Church. Not even Jewish mothers. The Church even has a rite of guiltage called the First Holy Communion.

I remember my First Holy Communion Day. All of the ladies were gushing, "Aw, how sweet!" and "Aw, how innocent!" They may have thought I was at the pinnacle of my innocence, but I knew that hereafter I would be pronounced guilty for doing the very same deeds that a day before had left me immaculately non-stigmatized.

Before I made my First Communion, I had to make my First Confession. To prepare for that, I had to learn a list of ten dos and don'ts, then go to confession and tell a priest about those I had violated. Actually, we confessed to breaking a commandment, not violating it. I think this breaking business all started with Moses, who broke the clay tablets containing the original command-ments. Since then, whenever we violate a law, a commandment, or a promise, we say we've broken it. Although we quite obvi-ously haven't, since they continue to work their guilt-tripping mojo just fine.

For the rest of my life I was supposed to go through that list, apply it to every deed I ever did, and determine where my guilt lay. No one ever suggested one could go through life sinless. A coma victim couldn't do it. To even think that I could, would be to commit the sin of presumption: the Church's version of Catch 22.

You might think that if one tried to be very righteous, one might alleviate some of this guilt. Not so. The Church has Catch 22A that not only makes the very guilty feel guilty, but the holier (less guilty) you become, the more guilty you feel.

This is called the doctrine of "Striving for Perfection."

Everyone is bound to it, but since no one can ever achieve it, everyone suffers guilty feelings for his or her shortcomings. The catch is that those feelings are in inverse proportion to the actual amount of guilt, because the closer you get to perfection, the more you realize how far you are from it, and therefore the guiltier you feel.

Many years ago, I was told by a priest that Catholics don't need psychiatric care as often as the rest of the populace because they have the confessional to unburden themselves. He must have been a Jesuit. They have a great fondness for offering extraneous criteria as proof of Catholicism's validity. I do remember that whoever said it offered no statistical proof. Such logic fails to consider that one might not be in such great need for the expiation found in the confessional or on the couch if so much guilt wasn't troweled onto one's psyche to begin with.

Not that I had any inkling of all that at the time. In fact, my First Confession went off without a hitch: there wasn't much to confess to, beyond the usual "I spit in my brother's milk so he wouldn't drink it and I could have it." A few Our Fathers and Hail Marys, and my cosmic slate was clean. Sadly, having communed with the Lord was not enough to keep me out of trouble. By the time I was eight or nine, it had become clear to me that I was a sinner. And I was likely to become more so, not less so.

Eve's Temptation: Anita lived in my neighborhood. We had been friends for all of our lives. She was a girl. I was not.

The Near Occasion of Sin: Our first excursion into sex, although we didn't know it was sex at the time, occurred when we were about six or younger. We watched each other pee.

The Occasion of Sin: At nine years old we knew nothing of love and little about sex, but we had unbridled curiosity. I was, therefore, able to talk an only slightly reluctant Anita into playing Doctor. She would lie down while I probed here and there, asking, "Does this hurt?" The longer we played the game, the more clothes were removed.

How could I ever confess that to a holy man—a man the nuns told us had forsaken sex forever? Certainly, this must be sex because it felt so good/so bad. Weeks went by, and the guilt intensified as I avoided the confessional.

Until this time, my greatest fear had been the same as my mother's, although I think my mother was a little more uptight about it; that I would get in an accident and the entire staff of the hospital would know that I hadn't changed my underwear. Of course, being a boy, the fear did not induce me to better my personal hygiene.

To make matters worse, I had procrastinated going to confession for so long that Anita and I had played Doctor again.

And again.

Finally, the guilt was too much and confession was the only answer.

The Confession

"ForgivemeFatherforIhavesinned. It has been four months since my last confession. In that time, I have taken the name of the Lord in vain eight times, talked back to my mother twice, and committed, mumble, mumble, once."

I reasoned that it was such a heinous crime that if I broke it up into three confessions, three weeks running, it would look far less despicable in his eyes.

"You committed *what*?"

"I committed adultery, Father."

"How, how, how many times?"

"ONCE! Father, only once!"

It was far worse than I had imagined. He was so disgusted with me that he put his head on his knees and covered his face with his hands. His shoulders shook convulsively as he cried. He stayed that way a long time. When he finally straightened up, I was mortified—more shamed than I had ever been in my life. He was so upset that as he lifted his head the tears streamed down his face while he...

...*laughed*? No, he wasn't just laughing—he was choking, trying to hold it in. After he calmed down to a few giggles now and then, he proceeded to ask me the most irrelevant, ridiculous questions imaginable.

"How old is she, Son?"

"My age, Father."

He started laughing all over again.

"Did you lie down next to her?"

Why would I want to do that?

"No, Father."

"Did you put anything into her?"

Now he had really lost me. What would I put into her? Where? Why?

"No, Father."

"Then what makes you think it was adultery?"

"Well, Father, the nuns taught me all sorts of ways to break the Ten Commandments. And Ani...um, I mean, the girl isn't married, so that means I couldn't be breaking "Thou Shalt Not Covet thy Neighbor's Wife." So I must be breaking "Thou Shalt Not Commit Adultery."

This explanation did nothing to subdue his mirth.

The Penance

I had to go through it all again the next week with a different priest, except this time, remembering my last confession, I admitted to the other two times. He kindly explained to me that it wasn't quite adultery—not yet, anyway. "Oh, I get it," I thought. "I dodged the bullet this time because I'm not old enough, but once I go through my Confirmation Day, my childhood innocence will be over, and I will become an adulterer by default."

A fellow should be so lucky...

8. The Eel and the Lantern

Once a year, the men of my family would go on a fishing trip to Grass Lake, wedged way up there in the upper reaches of Upstate New York, somewhere between Watertown and Alexandria Bay.

Quite often, I would team up with my Uncle Len. Len was a good fisherman, a superb raconteur, my godfather, my mentor, and since I was usually broke, my meal ticket. And I'll tell you this: the man caught fish. My father (his brother), always said that Len was just lucky. From this I formulated the hypothesis early on that when someone is always lucky, it isn't luck; it's skill.

When my son got old enough, he came with us. It was a joy to watch him giggle at my uncle's habit of singing the first stanza of *Diamonds Are a Girl's Best Friend*, over and over while he fished. And he thought his great uncle's favorite sayings and witticisms were hilarious.

When talking about someone he didn't admire, Len would say, "Ahhh he couldn't pour piss out of a boot if the directions were written on the heel." Or, "He's so dumb he has to be retrained every time he comes back from a piss break."

Uncle Len and I went into a bar after fishing one evening, and one of his friends asked, "How were they biting tonight, Len?"

He replied that we only caught a few.

The friend said, "You shoulda been here last night. You'd never guess how many we caught."

"Oh, I think I can," Len said. "Half."

"Half? Half of what?"

"Half of whatever you're going to tell me."

The thing that I remember most about him, besides his generosity and his folksy humor, was his infernal lantern. He had it all the years of my youth, and from the moment he brought it in the boat, it never failed to scare the living shit out of me. It made a low whistling hiss, as though it contained a nest of wasps. Its punctuation marks were sporadic flare-ups, when the sound would become that of an angry wasp nest with life-threatening potential. I always heard that sound as the precursor to my writhing, flaming death. One time it got to hissing and sputtering so loudly, I could barely hear my uncle as he chuckled, "Sounds like a cow pissing on a flat rock." I prayed often for the demonic thing to fall overboard.

Then there was the time Len and I, together with my eldest brother, were fishing in Aunt Betsy's Bass Hole. That was the name of Len's boat: Aunt Betsy's Bass Hole. Colorful, no? Anyway, my oldest brother caught an eel, which are voracious fish eaters. So he was determined not to release it to propagate more eels.

But he also didn't want to handle it.

Lowering it gingerly from his pole to the bottom of the boat, he attempted to chop off its head with a wooden oar, but the oar kept sliding off the slimy eel and clattering against the bottom of the boat. He raised the oar high overhead, and jabbed straight down at the neck of that serpent. And would you believe it? He succeeded—not in killing the eel, mind you—but in putting that oar straight through the bottom of Aunt Betsy's Bass Hole.

Poor Betsy erupted like a breaching whale, then began to sink. Going down, down, down, like the Edmund Fitzgerald, taking all three of us—and the slightly battered eel—with her.

After we swam ashore, I sauntered behind a covering bush, like I needed to take a leak and, unseen by my mates, I pumped my raised fist and did a brief victory jig, silently mouthing a triumphant "Yes, yes, yes!" You see, besides the fishing poles, nets, tackle boxes, clothes and other provisions, there was one more item lost to the deep that day. My nemesis—that infernal, diabolical, hissing lantern!

9. 'Twas Confiscation, Confound It!

"**A**ll right, young man! March right up here and put that sling-shot on my desk."

With that, Sister Disciplinus of the Order of Anything But Bleeding Hearts unlocked a desk drawer bulging with weaponry she had confiscated over the last hundred years. Once your possession entered her arsenal it never saw daylight again, except for the few brief seconds when the drawer would be opened to receive another piece of deadly military hardware.

"All right, Wormbreath! We think you're dealing drugs, so march right over here, and put the keys to that car, truck, plane, boat, whatever, in my hands." With that, Officer Cannibustya has just confiscated your vehicle, which you may see again—if the new owner lives nearby.

I know, I know. A lot of you are probably screaming that there's a big, big difference between the two cases. In the first example, it was the contraband that was taken; the mere possession of which was a violation of the rules. And in the second, the article confiscated was far removed from any possible crime. But I think dwelling on the differences puts up a smoke screen that hazes the similarities.

First and foremost of all, people who abuse the right to own property shouldn't complain when that right is denied them. Admit it: when you were a kid and did something foolish like letting the nun see your slingshot, you were angry with yourself, not with her, because you were guilty of breaking the Eleventh Commandment. You may have called her all of the dirty words in the Bible once she spied it, but you knew you had been stupid, and it was your own damn fault.

Likewise, allowing yourself to be suspected of dealing is stupid. Stopping when the cop tells you to is even more stupider.

Now you have a firm grasp on the first great similarity in the sample cases, i.e. stupidity.

Another great similarity exists in the economy of both cases. All governing agencies are being exhorted nowadays to streamline unnecessary labor costs. And in both of these instances, just that has been done. One person is the arresting officer, judge and jury. It don't get any leaner than that. My only problem is that I don't know why we're screwing around; if we're going to use 'streamline justice' to stop drugs, why don't we just shoot the dealers on the spot? Now, that would be *real* economics.

Another similarity between the two cases can be seen in the satisfaction derived by the nun and the cop. There is a little bit of jollies-getting-off in confiscating the prized possession of a scumbag. We all know that police officers suffer a lot of frustration in their work, and surely they deserve at least this little bit of a high. And, after all of the sacrifice she endures, isn't a nun entitled to a sacrificial lamb herself, now and then?

I can't wait until they make the law retroactive and start confiscating the property of anyone who has ever been suspected of breaking drug laws. Maybe it already is; after all, publishing all of the rules would take a lot of the fun out of it—for the arresting nun/officer, that is.

There's one more thing I want to say before you soft-on-criminal pansies start bleating too hard: you've already lost your virginity. The federal government has had legal means of confiscating your property without due process of law for years. They call it income tax.

At least Sister Disciplinus only took our slingshots.

10. Truant False

When I was growing up, skipping school was a cardinal sin. It simply *was not done*, and if it was done by anyone anywhere, it wasn't done by anyone anywhere near our house. That's because my mother considered it a *mortal* sin. Of course, I didn't think of that on that long ago yesterday when I committed the familial felony. For a boy in the eighth grade, consequences simply do not exist.

So I skipped.

The next morning I faked a note from my mother excusing me from school the day before. When I got to class I handed it to my teacher. But Sister Mary Decrepitude of the Order of Hoarders reached into her desk drawer, rummaged around, and came up with a real note from my mother that my elder sister had turned in years before.

"Master Belge, the note you gave me was not signed by your mother. I want you to go home and bring me one that is."

Oh boy! I thought. Go tell Mother that I lied to the teacher? That was another thing one did not do. Not in our house. In our house, the consequences for skipping school were the worst, but the consequences for lying were even worser. And for lying to a nun, my friends, there was none worse.

When I got home there was no one there. So I sat and waited to face the worst punishment of my life. I remember thinking, boy, my mother is going to kill me three times over. I contemplated my mortality, wondering how much more dead than dead I could get. I didn't know and I didn't want to find out.

So I came up with a brilliant New Plan. I wrote a new note, adding a long list of punishments that my mother would administer to correct my lying, forging, school-skipping ways. And this time, I took pains to do a better job with the signature.

Back I went to school the next day, fresh note in hand. Sister

Mary D. raised an eyebrow and said, "Master Belge, I do not know whom you are trying to fool, but this is not your mother's handwriting!"

"I know, Sister," I said in a downtrodden voice of surrender. "But she was doing the wash, and she told me what to write and then she dried her hands and signed it."

I waited nervously while she inspected the signature. Just as I'd hoped, her eye was more taken by the list of punishments my mother intended to visit upon me. Sister's face lit with a smile that said, "There, you little heathen. After all the crap you've given me, you're finally getting a steaming pile of your own."

She was both right and wrong—I deserved it, but I did not get it. Not that time, anyway...

11. Oneupmanship

'Twas the day after Christmas and my gang of friends and I were in our usual spot, loitering on the stoop of the local soda shop. We had two younger fellows in our neighborhood, Happy and John, whom we often let tag along with us. They were best friends but they were always trying to outdo each other.

This particular day each approached us from different directions at the same time and each of them had a big grin plastered on his face.

As soon as they met, John started bragging about all of his Christmas gifts. Just when Happy thought he was finished, John unzipped his jacket and displayed his greatest prize, a woolen sweater with a big deer embroidered across the chest. His big grin got even bigger, believing that Happy could not top that.

Now it was Happy's turn. He listed gift after gift, but John just smiled on, confident that his sweater was the winner. At the end of his litany of largess, Happy went in for the kill—and held out his arm to display a brand-new wrist watch!

John's smile faded as he realized he was bested by a grown person's gift; a watch, a symbol of responsibility and sophistication.

Then his face lit up again.

"What time is it?" he asked, grinning from ear to ear.

Happy, undaunted, smiled back at him and offered his arm saying, "Why don't you see for yourself?"

Poor John's last, best gambit had failed. For it was true that Happy hadn't yet mastered the art of telling time—but then again, neither had John.

12. Wheelman

I was eighteen with a brand new driver's license and bragging all over town. Manny was sixteen, and his brother, "The Greek," was about fifteen. Neither had a license, so they had come to me. They were in a jam: the boys had "borrowed" their father's car to go for a joyride. Their father had seen the car turn a corner, but he hadn't seen who was driving. So, to get out from under, they told him that they had conned me into driving by telling me that they had his permission. He didn't believe them, so he told them to get me to prove it.

The boys and I sat on the couch. Their father sat facing us with the mother standing behind her husband. I did my best, but confessing to being their wheel-man did nothing for their father. He ranted on and on for hours, getting angrier and angrier with each succeeding minute. All I could think of was an apoplectic Adolph rabidly haranguing his thoroughly propagandized crowds. Spittle kept flying from Manny's dad's mouth as he raged. Halfway through his diatribe, I was drenched.

At the pique of his rage, he threatened to call the police and swear out warrants against us, assuring us that spending a few nights in a cell would do us a world of good.

If there was a Sucker of the Year Award—or if there had been Darwin Awards back then—I would have taken first prize. I believed every syllable he uttered. Sitting there, quaking in my sneakers, I wondered how in Heaven's name I had got myself into such a cluster-flock. But more importantly, how was I going to explain it to my parents and make them believe that I wasn't even in the car, without ratting on my friends?

Just as I was about to give up the ghost, jump ship, and spill the beans, I noticed his wife standing behind him, looking at the three of us, shaking her head "no" and shrugging her shoulders at each dire threat her husband so spittingly proclaimed.

The threat of jail seemed to be his parting salvo, and thanks to his wife we already knew which way this was going. He ended up sending me off with one last wag of his finger, and a stern warning that if such a thing ever happened again, my parents and I would never hear the end of it.

I thanked God and my lucky stars all the way home that I was not in jail. There's a good chance my father would have agreed that a night in the slammer would serve me right. And I doubted my mother had enough "cookie jar money" to post my bail—if she were so inclined—which was equally doubtful.

13. Fear of Heights

S ome guys look at life in the military through olive-drab glasses; they romanticize it. I, on the other hand, look at it with a jaundiced eye.

Probably because I'm yellow, through and through.

So when I was mustered out of service, I knew I wanted no more of the military life. Nothing could entice me to re-up. No sir! Two weeks in the Boy Scouts were more than enough.

Thus, I knew joining the military for real was not for me when I matriculated high school. "Matriculated"—sounds like a bunch of drips seeped through the school grounds, doesn't it? Well, in my case that wasn't too far off the mark.

When I was ten or so, my friends and I saw "Sergeant York," starring Gary Cooper as a green recruit, bringing in a whole platoon (company? division?) of enemy soldiers on his own. Kicking the mud from his boots, he drawled, "Gee General, wunt no even fight; alls they had war a bunch of itty-bitty cannons agin my Winchester!" This scene impressed my friends.

It impressed me too, but in a different way. A lot of people like to daydream about what their lives would be like had they been born during the Middle Ages. They envision themselves as a Knight of the Round Table or as a princess, perhaps. What chutzpah! By what right do they dream so? My friends and I were born to factory worker fathers, not kings or heads of state. So if I were born in an earlier age, sure as Galahad's gauntlets, I wouldn't have been the guy who entered the locked chambers of the fair maiden; I would have been the serf who emptied the fair maiden's chamber pot.

Thinking thusly, I visualized myself not as Sergeant York, but as one of the many Germans he killed, whose deaths served the grand and glorious purpose of scaring the shite out of the German platoon/company/division–whatever–so they would surrender. Yup, sure as yer shootin', I wouldn't have been a hero or an officer. I would've been cannon fodder.

Maybe I should stop here, before I paint myself with too pastel a brush. I've never been in a fight-or-die situation, so who knows how I would react? I hope I would be a hero, even if I don't want to be an officer—or a gentleman.

After all, I wouldn't want you to think that here stands a man with a soul so dead that he never in his youth dared his friends to go up to the round-top on Lincoln Park Hill and sneak peeks at couples making out in their cars. Which we did. And it was great until one of the maker-outers spied us spying on him.

Now, *that* was an unnerving experience. I ask you now, as we asked each other then, "What's he gonna do about it? He can't chase us with no pants on!" And again, I ask you now, as we asked each other moments later, "How the hell'd he get his pants on so fast?" (Note to future self: they were only down to his ankles, that's how.) In six-point-four nanoseconds a not-so-jolly giant was breathing fire down our collective neck's nape. I was so scared I raced off a six-foot stone wall with my feet still pedaling in the air like Wile E. Coyote—when I landed, I was already running.

There was a bonus: the jolt of suddenly rejoining the earth made me sneeze out the loose teeth Romeo had jammed up my nasal passages.

It's important to me that you understand one thing—just because I was terrified of death and didn't think the military life was for me, didn't mean I was a strictly non-adventurous boob. Oh, I was a boob—but I had adventures. Sometimes I was even foolish enough to initiate them myself. Like when Slatz, the Fonzie of St. Vincent de Paul High, described his exhilarating life as a climber for the Davey Tree Company, heroically clipping off the tree branches that threatened to impinge on poor, defenseless power lines. I immediately signed on, despite the fact that I was terrified by heights—even more scared than I was by the military, or death.

I found that you can overcome that fear. It takes time and

guts, but it can be done. And I value the process I went through as one of the most exhilarating, adventurous periods of my life. But that's now. Back then, when I was scared witless ninety percent of the time, it was more of a never-ending, waking nightmare.

During the first couple of weeks, my co-workers thought that I was in love with every tree that I climbed. I hugged those trunks so tightly my chest and stomach looked like I was the seaman caught stealing Captain Queeg's strawberries—as though I'd been roped up, thrown overboard, and hauled across the keel.

I remember the time my boss tried to convince me that it was possible to stand on a telephone cable—located halfway up the fifty-foot pole—and by leaning my shoulder into the pole, free my hands so that I could strap on a tool-belt. First of all, telephone cables are not at all taut—they're not even tutored a little. What they are is slack, and they move under your feet. I'm also prepared to swear on a Bible that once you have both hands free of the pole, it too becomes wishy-washy, and offers about as much purchase as an uninflated inflatable doll floating in a swimming pool of honey. After several tries, the boss gave up on ever teaching me that maneuver—probably because he was standing right under me with my tool-belt on his head.

Once I got used to the wuthering heights, a thought occurred to me: why is an oversized log, installed and maintained by the electric company and dominated by a network of electrical wires that only has one telephone cable on the whole bloody thing called a telephone pole? Hm?

By the way, before you get any clever ideas about enlisting my aid to paint the upper reaches of your house, let me tell you that acrophobia is like herpes; long after you're sure you're cured, it comes back with a vengeance.

14. Dey Brothers!

When I was a freshman at LeMoyne College in Syracuse, New York, I had a part-time job at Brothers Department Store. And what a job it was! Most of the stockers were high-school students and had to be closely supervised. As a man of experience—I'd graduated high school *months* ago—I saw an opportunity. I approached several of the buyers and floor managers with the same proposition—give me the amount of work usually done by two stockers in a four-hour shift, tell me exactly how you want it done, and I'll do it and do it right.

What a sweet job! It didn't take more than a couple of days for them to see that I was as good as my word. And that gave me the autonomy I was looking for. So I'd work my butt off for the first two hours—and spend the next two roving throughout the store, practicing my charm on the salesgirls and clerks. One of these was fast becoming my girlfriend.

Let me explain the mystique of the downtown location. Those of you who remember the song "Downtown," (*When you're alone and life is making you lonely, you can always go...Downtown!*) need no explanation. Those of you who don't remember the song, do.

You see, in the first half of the last century, Downtown was the place to be for an upscale, trendy store. Oh, you could open a store in one of the finer neighborhoods or in one of the suburbs, but never all three like they do now.

Three? What am I talking about? Nowadays, there are thirty-seven Starbucks on my block alone, for crying out loud.

As I was saying, Downtown was where it was at, man. All the big players in the retail game had their flagship locations, either along Main Street, or as Main Street-adjacent as they could get. I'm talking Woolworth's and Lerner's and...oh, hell; if you don't remember the song, you don't remember those, either, do you?

You'll just have to take my word that there was a certain

panache in working at the downtown stores. Besides that, there were perks—like a company softball team. It was on that team that I met a guy named Wilbur, and we quickly became buddies. You'll wonder why in a minute, but he was a great athlete, a very important trait in my adulating, youthful eyes.

Wilbur had a problem with girls and his problem was this: no matter what a girl actually said—"hello" for instance—what Wilbur *heard* was "Your manliness drives me wild with desire." His attempts to reply in kind consistently failed to produce the desired result, but Wilbur never caught on that he was his own worst enemy.

So it came as no surprise to anyone but Wilbur that he still had no date for the fast-approaching New Year's Eve party at the Hotel Syracuse. In a last-ditch effort to find a date, he asked my girlfriend if she had a sister he could take out for the celebration. She said she didn't have a sister, but she did have a friend, her best friend, who would go with him.

"Her best friend?" I thought to myself. Couldn't she bring some schlub of a friend she barely knew, someone she wouldn't worry too much about if things went wrong? No, it had to be her best friend, Sally. I sensed trouble.

But before we get to that, I fear I must diffuse the story by digressing once more.

If you grew up in Syracuse, you may remember the expression *"Dey Brothers!"* It was shorthand for, "If what you just said turns out to be true, I'll kiss your ass in Dey Brothers' display window!" Over time, it became an all-purpose exclamation of derision or disagreement. So instead of saying, "What? Superman, get Lois pregnant?" you simply cried, *"Dey Brothers!"* and everyone knew what you meant.

Which brings us back to Wilbur.

What Wilbur didn't know was that due to his aforementioned girl problem, the likelihood of him having a really great date on New Year's Eve—or any other eve, for that matter—was definitely *"Dey Brothers!"*

When I delicately pointed this out to him, he told me in no uncertain terms that I was wrong, dead wrong.

"Artie," he said, "You are wrong, dead wrong. I'm gonna get to second base with Sally on New Year's Eve, guaranteed."

"*Dey Brothers!*" I exclaimed in true, sarcastic Syracusan fashion.

"Done!" he said without missing a beat.

"Done?" I asked.

"Yes. I accept your challenge."

"What challenge?" I queried.

"If I don't get to second base with Sally, I will kiss your ass in Dey Brothers' window."

"Sounds good to me. I'll bring the popcorn."

"Whoa, whoa, whoa, Artie," he said. "You realize that if I *do* get to second base, *you'll* have to kiss *my* ass in Dey Brothers' window."

This was such a sure bet, I almost called Dey Brothers on *his* Dey Brothers—doubling down on a derrière, as it were. ("I double-dog derrière ya!")

But now, I really digress.

New Year's Eve arrived, as hotly awaited as this return to the subject, and the four of us headed downtown to the Hotel Syracuse. Let me tell you, this party was as close to top-shelf as Syracuse got, and they charged a buttload for it—each ticket cost as much as we made in a week. Wilbur—being Wilbur—figured that shelling out all that money would so impress Sally, that she would be moved to...appreciate his largesse with a bit of hanky-panky.

So it was, when midnight came and the people cheered and the bells rang and the noise-makers noised, he tried for a midnight kiss. But Sally turned her head, offering only her cheek. "I promised Mother not to kiss boys on the first date. Please don't be angry."

Oh, but Wilbur *was* angry.

The party ended soon after. We all piled into my car and set out to drop Sally at her house, with Wilbur sulking the whole way. I figured he'd given up, but, no; he'd merely been calculating his last, best move.

"I suppose," he said to Sally as she backed out of the car. "I suppose if I couldn't get a New Year's kiss, then a good night fuck is out of the question."

"Not at all," said Sally, "Good night, *Fuck.*"

My girlfriend laughed. Wilbur wilted. I hit the gas.

Next stop—*Dey Brothers!*

15. Dey Brothers, Too

If you use the expression, *"Dey Brothers!"* ten years from now—even to a native Syracusan—I'm afraid people will stare at you the way they stare at me...whenever I speak. Dey Brothers Department Store is gone, an era has passed.

As for myself, nothing will ever replace Dey Brothers. Not in my heart, and not in my vocabulary. I don't mean Dey Brothers itself, I mean the expression. We can live without the store, but the loss of the expression is going to be a severe cultural set-back for a town already so culturally deprived that the best eating spot is a hamburger stand in the lobby of its majorly dilapidated major hotel.

In addition to my triumph as a stockboy, I also did a stint in sales at Dey's. They asked me to work the floor on a Saturday during a bargain basement sale.

Men, if you've never been to such a sale, keep it that way. All of the things you've seen in movies and cartoons are true. The meekest and mildest of women turn into watered gremlins—absolutely vicious. (What is the proper term for a group of gremlins, I wonder. A "growl"? A "grisly"? Ooh, how about "a *gruesome*"?)

Anyway, on the occasion of the bargain sale, the older salesladies "worked the floor," augmented by us part-timers. I was surprised to find that the salesladies all stuck close to their counters, never venturing beyond them. If someone brought stuff up to the counter, well, fine—they'd ring it up. But there was no way any one of them would play the brave warden during a prison uprising and actually step out into that throng.

But I was more brave than bright, so I sailed right onto the floor and sold, sold, sold. When the day ended, I had sold more than twice as much as my nearest runner-up. But the ladies were not pleased, matter of fact, they were mightily miffed.

What I hadn't known as a part-timer who was paid hourly,

was that the full-timers were paid hourly—*plus commission*. In one afternoon I went from being, "that chubby, well-mannered, young man working in the stockroom," to, "that fat, smart-alec stockboy who stole our commissions."

Monday morning, I happily returned to the safety of my stockroom where I found solace with one of the more easily impressed younger sales-lasses. She actually insisted I take her out! So after work, we went to Heid's and shared a coney dog, and we snuggled; then we took a romantic drive to the lake, and when we parked, she kissed me! On the lips! Then it was time for the submarine races to start, as the sun, like my date, slowly sank, slipping from view...

Dey Brothers!

16. Prostitute Teacher

"Arthur, Aaarthur, Aaaaarthur..." My mother intones from her place in Heaven. (Mothers never call you "Artie" when they're upset with you; ever notice that?)

"You are a substitute, substitute, substi-tu-u-ute." (Ghostly apparitions always warmup by saying things three times. Why is that? Huh? Why, I ask you? Why?)

"I know being a substitute has you prostate right now," she continues. "But I don't think you realize how naughty you're being when you call yourself a prosti...that other thing. It's naughty, Arthur, naughty, naughty, *naaaaughty*."

Well, now! There are all sorts of things that I want to say in my defense, but I'm in a bind—a couple of binds, in fact. First of all, you can't argue with a mother who is in Heaven—especially now she's practically running the place. Furthermore, I have no intention of helping her distinguish between "being prostrate" and "having a prostate." I tried once before, but the debate devolved once again into the age-old tentacle cum testicle debacle. Ewww!

Take the matter of classroom discipline. The students usually behave better for the regular teacher because they know the teacher is going to be there all year. They know he'll be in touch with their parents if there are any problems, and that he holds the ultimate power over their final grades.

The prostitu....er, *prostrated* teacher has none of these weapons. The sub doesn't even have the option of sending students to the office. We have the threat, but not the weapon. Principals will tell you that if you have a problem with a student, by all means, send them to the office. But if you do, the principal will label you "weak"—and advise the person who is in charge of assigning subs not to call you in the future.

"Send 'em to Detention!" you say. But because of busing, most schools don't have detention anymore. I sure wish it was like that when I was in school. I had so many detentions in eighth grade, I still hadn't served them all when I graduated from college ten years later. I still have nightmares with Sister Mary Rached towing me back to school by my ear to complete my sentence.

There are good times to be had as a substitute teacher, too. Recently I taught a second grade class and had a ball. When giving them a spelling test, I used the words in alliterative sentences:

"Flew. The fat falcon flew fast. Flew."

Their giggles made the effort worthwhile. A couple of them didn't remember how many days there were in the month. So we went over the jingle. Do you remember it? "Thirty days hath Septober, April, Alice and No wonder; all the rest have thirty-some, except the Grand Canyon, it has cactus plants." Nobody forgets that one.

Except for me. When I was in second grade, a mean old car broke my arm just because I was sledding in its right-of-way. While I was out of school, the rest of the class learned the months of the year. When I returned I was horribly embarrassed that I didn't know something the other kids knew. That horrible embarrassment lasted until the eighth grade, when one day I found out that I had somehow learned them by osmosis. Talk about lack of academic curiosity—it never occurred to me during all those years to take five minutes with a calendar.

I guess I preferred embarrassment to enlightenment.

My godson, Porter, has been doing substitute work in Oswego, New York. His first classroom stint was monitoring kindergärteners. One little girl hid under a small table. No matter how he coaxed, she would not come out. The student consiglieri of the class advised him that "When she *does* come out, she runs out of the school and doesn't come back!" Porter left her under the table.

On another occasion he was reading a story to a sixth grade class. The story said that one character had long johns on. A couple of the girls wanted to know what long johns were. One boy said, "I know! I know! Let me tell them!" Porter told the boy to go ahead. "Men wear them," the boy said, "to cover their peckers."

"What's a pecker?" one of the girls asked. "Never mind," Porter said as his face reddened, "let's get on with the story."

That story reminded me of an experience during my second year teaching, long before I became a proselytizing restaurateur. It was the first week of a new school year, and my first year in the Syracuse School System. I was teaching a geography unit on Hawaii to a group of high school students. One young lady said she and her family had lived in Hawaii when her father was stationed there. She had a large coral collection, hula records, a hula dancer's outfit and many pictures. Would I like her to bring these things in to share with the class? "Most certainly," said I.

I entered class the following day to find the students all gathered around a large table in the front of the room, examining a display of coral and picture albums of the Islands. Hula music was coming from a record player. The owner of these treasures was demonstrating hula movements and explaining what each of them meant. Wearing a long flowing muumuu, she really looked the part.

Wow, this was terrific! That is, until she whipped off the muumuu, disclosing the briefest of bikinis I had ever seen. I mean, there was almost no bikini at all—the young lady was showing more skin than a Thanksgiving turkey.

And then she began to dance the hula for true-la, which, as it turns out, is quite an erotic style of dance.

Now, like my good friend Walter Cronkite, I must ask you to travel back in time with me to that long ago yesteryear, when what was considered to be acceptable behavior was far different than 'tis now. I mean, I'm not sure I'd feel comfortable if I found myself in that same situation today, but a half a century ago it was definitely verboten, taboo and otherwise looked down and frowned upon.

It took me a couple of minutes, but I finally got Miss Hawaii and the rest of the class in some semblance of order. And none too soon, because the principal stalked through the door, demanding to know "what this *ruckus* is all about!"

I prostated myself before God, the principal, the students and everybody, but before I could think of a plausible lie or suitable bribe to get me off the hook, I heard my mother again, haranguing me from her Heaven perch.

"*Ar-thur.   A-a-arthur.   Aaaaaarthur!*   Stop   prostituting yourself..."

17. 1929 Buick in Near-Mint Condition

Back in '57 (*1957*, smart-ass) I was in graduate school, putting the finishing touches on knowing everything.* A friend who'd heard I was in the market for a car told me about an elderly gentleman who had one for sale.

I went to take a look. As we were walking from the owner's house to his garage, he explained that he only used the car to go to the A&P for groceries every second Thursday. Every first Thursday, he would start it up and let it run for a few minutes to keep the engine from seizing up. Except during the winter, that is, when he only started it up once a week, because he had it up on blocks and didn't drive it at all.

I didn't believe a word.

He opened up the garage door, and wow, what a gorgeous machine! A 1929 Buick in near-mint condition. It was jet black with a square body. The headlights were mounted on thin shafts on well-defined fenders. The center of the roof was patent leather, black. The tan seat covering was wool. It was kinda itchy—but hey, if itchy wool was the in-thing in '29, well, that was good enough for me!

The only real drawback was it would need tires soon; not because the ones on it were worn, but because they were starting to crack. They were the original tires and were drying out from age.

I offered him seventy-five dollars, my tongue lolling out of the side of my mouth. While this was five dollars more than I had ever paid for a car, I knew it was at least $125 short of what he was probably asking. He hemmed and hawed, and eventually said he wanted $100. I hawed and hemmed, and we settled halfway at $87.50.

I washed, waxed, and polished that car. People would stop to look at it parked in the road in front of our apartment. Several offered to buy it—one man offered me $400! It was obvious I was one of the sharpest businessmen in town.

After a few days of that, I began to wonder just how much this fine classic car was really worth. I decided to take it to a Buick dealer and find out.

Please do not consider that I was twenty-four years old; nor that I had a business degree and was working on a masters. Nor that I was married, had children and was supporting them without scholarships, student loans or the GI Bill. Please do not consider those factors, because they make me sound quite mature, when actually I was living in an age far less mature than young people live in today. I was the epitome of that age: cocky, self-assured, totally wet behind the ears—and too naïve to know it.

The salesman at the dealership said, "We don't handle antique autos here."

"I'll take care of this, Jim!" cut in the owner of the dealership, elbowing his salesman out of the way.

That's when I should have smelled a rat.

He put his hand on my shoulder and drew a smiling breath—the last breath he drew for the next forty-five minutes as he talked non-stop.

"You do realize that having mechanical brakes hurts its resale value?" he opportuned.

Pssst, another aside here. Have you ever noticed the hand-painted sign in front of the garage on State Street that reads "Mehniac on Duty"? I always thought you'd have to be crazy to take your car there.

"Sure!" I said. Well, I really didn't, because I didn't know diddly about car mechanics. I did know that the car stopped just fine, if you put both feet on the pedal, pressed real hard, and arched your back.

"And even if you can find a mechanic who is old enough to remember how to repair it, which is doubtful, you can't get parts for this baby anymore."

But anyone who knows more than I do about cars, which

is to say most of humanity, knows how thoroughly I was being BS-ed — the only vehicle simpler to fix would be a unicycle. A standard screwdriver, pliers and adjustable wrench would suffice to effect 95% of all repairs. Some of you old-timers out there, which is to say, that small sliver of humanity who are older than I, will remember the amazingly simple Ford wrench, it was supposed to fit every single nut on their cars.

I believed every word.

The salesman waltzed me out to the lot and led me to one of his cars. "I can see you have a sharp mind for business, Mr. Belge. Now, here's a car you can drive while you advertise it for resale, and make some bucks on it. Sharp guy like you, you'll sell it quick! And when you sell it to the new owner, you ask him to drop you off right here, and I'll fix you up with another one. You won't have to *work* your way through college: you're going to *sell* your way through college! Because, like I say, you have a sharp mind for business, doncha, son?"

By the time he was finished with me, I had dollar signs in my eyes. I eagerly traded in my beautiful Buick for a used Studebaker taxicab that was so beat up it would make a demolition derby loser look like a shiny new floor model. But I didn't care — it was an investment. I was going to make a mint selling used cars!

As I drove off, it slowly came to me that the sharpest businessman in town had just crossed blades with Syracuse's answer to Zorro...and lost.

Regarding knowing everything, my brother had a friend who studied medicine to become a general practitioner. When he completed that, he went back to school to specialize in internal medicine. And after that, he decided to further refine his field of knowledge to ears, nose and throat. "You know," he said, "if I keep narrowing down my specialty, pretty soon I'll know all there is to know about nothing!"

Spoil-Sport

1. Gin Rummies

Life with Jack is never boring. When it comes to recreation, he has great ideas. I remember one night in particular, he was really on a roll. We had just been asked to leave our usual haunt for getting a bit too rowdy, so we were looking for a diversion. That's when he came up with his first Big Idea.

I'd better not go into all the details, but it involved several pink flamingos and a gallon of baby oil. For the record, I'm against baby oil, considering the source. When the flamingo fiasco went up in flames he devised his Second Big Idea, we would go to a wine tasting. Hmm, never been to one of those before. Why not?

As soon as we got there I said, "This dance is gonna be a drag." I said over and-a over and-a over again, "This dance is gonna be a drag." I mean when you're talking about Jack and me, you're talking about two guys who think a high-stepping night out is dinner at Heid's Hot Dog Stand, three lines of open bowling, and a string of visits to our favorite barmaids.

Yet there we were, in some fancy-schmancy place, listening to some affected arsehole spout off about the three A's: Acidity, Astringency and Smell. Thank goodness our bowling shirts were clean—well, they were when we started out—or we might have felt out of place.

We decided to skedaddle. But before we left we stuffed our pockets with little packets of crackers, grabbed a couple of fistfuls of cheese, and said, "Hey, it's been grape, mon sherry, brut we're heading for another port in just a sec."

And wouldn't you know it, there was a bona-fide rathskeller not two doors down.

"Alright! Let's try this wine seller's wine-cellars, fellers!" Jack ejaculated.

"We are conducting a gin tasting tour, innkeeper, so two tots of your finest grain spirits, sil voo play," Jack snooted.

The bartender smirked as he hoisted the Boodles and poured us each a double.

"It is perturbingly slight on nose, but it most positively has body," Jack declared.

"I know what you mean. One of its elbows just jabbed me in the throat," I croaked.

"Sommelier, something from a loftier shelf, if you please," I whispered hoarsely.

Two Chatham gins appeared before us.

"We might have something here," I said. "Chatham is in England, and who knows gin better than the Brits?"

With one sip, Jack coughed and cried, "You're talking about the people who eat kidney pie, the people who boil their beef! At least now we know what they do with the beef broth after they get done tanning leather with it!"

"But didn't you notice the fruity character?"

"He isn't bothering you, leave him alone," Jack replied. "I'm talking about this sheep dip. It should come with a warning label: Hazardous Waste."

"Yaws, veddy good," I agreed in a nasal tone emanating from my recently burned nasal toner, "definitely flinty."

Having, with two drinks, sampled the full range of the rathskeller's gin inventory, we decided to move upward, then onward to other peeling plaster palaces.

The next whiskey warden kept a much classier place. You noticed it in subtle ways, like the larger assortment of gin and the velvet Elvis completely covering the back bar.

We found Barron's gin without nose and definitely immature; or maybe it was just that the bartender had a quick wrist and thick-bottomed shot glasses. I mentioned this to a guy next to me, and he said, "Sam's doing you a favor. Nobody in their right mind wants enough of that shit so that they can actually taste it."

Crystal Palace was OK, but no bouquet, well maybe a small corsage. On a scale of four roses, I'd give it one petal. Couldn't compare to a lusty Liebfraumilch though—it was more like a frigid Fraulein.

We found the Beefeater to be stone-faced; the Boodles had oodles of sass; and the Tanqueray was obviously from a jealous year. All three were actually quite rich. Rich, I tell ya! Rich, rich, rich! And by rich I mean FOUR FREAKIN' BUCKS A POP!

"Sam," I slurred, "bring down that Crystal Palace bottle again. I think it may have some hidden nuances that we missed on the first go-round."

One thing we noted about all the gins we sampled: none of them had what the critics called "legs"—unless they were referring to the petrified caterpillar at the bottom of the last bottle we sampled.

On the way out, Jack suggested that we go back to our home bar and beg the owner to let us back in. Best idea yet!

2. Coach Potato

*S*everal years ago, the female *habitués* of our local upholstered sewer formed a softball team. And there I stood, beer glass in hand, voicing my approval—a luxury that I could easily afford, since, except for the fact that my wife Starr was going to play, I would have nothing to do with it. I mean, they had a coach, a team, and a sponsor. The only place that I fit in was cheering on the sidelines, right?

Sweet *naiveté.*

It wasn't until we were driving home that Starr happened to mention that Coach Sandy was going to need an assistant. "Someone who knows a lot about the game," she said. Then she added in the most *sotto* of voices, "...so I told him you would do it."

Being a wiser guy than I, it only took Coach Sandy a few practices to realize with "regret, much regret" that the demands of his regular job, unfortunately "so unfortunately"—necessitated his resignation from the team.

Before I knew it, I was drafted as head coach. It was a blatant case of tete fiat, and it was my tete that was being fiatted.

There I stood, ball in hand, with nary a clue what to do next.

Put yourself in my cleats. Throughout my youth, summers were spent on the softball field. I was familiar with the rules and the rudiments. I knew which end of the stick (in theory, at least) was used to hit the ball over the fence, and why a ball player worked to develop the pocket in his glove. (So the ball doesn't slosh out and bonk him on the nose. Of course, we all know there are no guarantees in this life.) I was soon to learn, however, that knowing the language doesn't automatically make you a capable translator.

It's easy to see that Mary swings her bat like Lizzie Borden; Sally uses her glove as a shield; Alice throws the ball like it's a rotten tomato; Betty runs like Tom Selleck is chasing her and she would love to get caught, and all of them think *slide* is Japanese for *drop right where you are and stay put*. While it was easy for me to spot these errors, I had no experience in their correction.

My solution was to step away and go through sliding into base, or stopping a ground ball, or whatever, in slow-motion while I paid attention to what my body was doing. My slow-mo ballet was often accompanied by a perplexed expression, and the players would sometime ask me what I was doing—thinking maybe I'd contracted some exotic nerve disease. Because I didn't want to admit how inept I was, I usually muttered something like, "...cold in my hip...working out the kinks..."

Coaching is hard work. It is demanding, challenging, time-consuming, and frustrating. But there *are* compensations— rewards, even. Obviously, there's the thrill of winning. But with or without winning, there's also the satisfaction of seeing the players develop as your advice and training sink in. Following are a few examples of my coacherly wisdom, and how the players made it their own.

"Follow through! Follow through!" I would cry to the batters, fielders or runners to first. Is there any sport in the world where coaches do not holler "follow through"?

Mary learned to follow through. On one swing she popped the ball up about two feet, and her follow-through was so complete that the bat came around behind her and hit the ball a second time—right down the third base line! I stood there dumbfounded—and so, for a moment, did the umpire, who had already called "strike one!" the first time Mary's bat connected. Would he change his ruling to "fair ball"—or maybe even "strike *two*"?

"SSStill ssstrike one!" the ump stammered, tears rolling down his cheeks.

"When the first basewoman goes for the ball, the pitcher or second basegirl (she was only 16) must cover first base."

On one such play, both players covered first. The first basewoman, however, was able to field the ball and return to first before the batter got there. The crowd roared, all seventeen of them, while the three players crammed themselves on top of the base and handed the ball back and forth.

"Once the ball is hit, fielders should never be standing still; there is always someplace they are needed as back-up."

It was a high pop fly. The woman playing second base went back, while the right and left center fielders came in—and all converged on the ball. "Out! No! Out! No! Out! No! Out!" cried the ump, as the ball popped from glove to glove to glove and back into the original fielder's glove.

How *do* you score that one? Is it a double or triple assist?

"If a ground ball is going to go foul, and you have time to grab it and put the runner out, do so. Otherwise, let it go foul."

The ball hit the ground in front of home plate and then bounced high. The pitcher got to the first baseline as it came down. Toeing the baseline with both feet, Edna leaned over the line, doing little pinwheels with her hands to keep her balance. In an act of perfect coordination, she stabbed her glove under the ball, pirouetted without entering foul territory, and threw the ball to first before the runner got there. Well, we all knew it was one of the greatest plays we had ever seen—if we were playing basketball or football. But what was it in baseball? "Foul ball!" the ump correctly called.

"You don't have to touch the runner on a force out; just touch the base."

Mary learned that. (This is not the same Mary previously cited. One of the first things a coach learns is that the fates dictate that in order to promote confusion, every team must have either three people with the same first name, or two sets of people with the same first names. This rule, of course, also applies to last names—but in reverse.) Mary fell, stopping a hard grounder over second. She then crawled to the base, reached out, and set the ball on the base.

When the ump finally stopped laughing, she said: "If you wanna let me know when you're done building that monument, I'll gladly call the runner out."

But I have to admit when all is said and done, the love of the players and the respect of the fans make it all worth...Wait! Am I out of my effing mind? The best players will make errors because what you're hollering at them doesn't mean squat to them, because they know better than you. The worst players always believe they're *not* the worst, and deserve more field time. And even if there are only six fans, each one will tell you six different things you did wrong, and none of them is right.

But seriously, now that the season has ended, we're having a little get-together at a local pub. The team has asked me to give a speech. I think I have a pretty good start on it:

It is with regret—much, much regret...

3. A True Fisherman...

I love fishing. I enjoy everything connected with it: fresh air, boating, sunshine, skinny-dipping, and those rare occasions when I actually land a keeper. Oh, yes—and the lies. I love the lies. Lying is the best part of fishing, and as integral to the sport as the bean ball is to baseball.

Lie about your golf score or bowling average, and deep down you have an unclean feeling, akin to the disgust you (should) feel when you cheat at solitaire. But a true fisherman never feels a twinge of guilt. A true fisherman considers lying about the sport to be as much of a sport as the sport itself. A true fisherman never tells the truth when a whopper will suffice.

A true fisherman is a born liar.

All the more so because he knows that after telling the lie for the third time, the Fisherman's Triple Negative Rule comes into effect. From then on, he is fully entitled to believe his own lie.

The way it works is this. The first time he tells it, it's a bald-faced lie. The second time, he adds some interesting details that actually happened—and now the lie becomes a mere punch line to those details. The third time, he adds a number of colorful sidelights that could have happened, or actually did happen at another time—and the original lie is merely an obscure focal point around which an interesting yarn is built. And everybody loves a good yarn.

Thereafter, fact and fiction become so interwoven and irrelevant that, by golly, that's *exactly* the way it happened.

St. Peter would never have called Ananias a liar if he had confined himself to fish stories. Ananias, by the way, dropped dead on the spot. And you thought your mom was tough when she said, "Don't lie to me or it will go hard with you!" After all, having been a fisherman, Peter must have liked a good yarn. He more than likely would have just waited for Ananias to finish talking so he could tell *his* story about the time he hauled in a net-full when everyone said the Dead Sea was. Or how he was not only the best dancer on the cast-a-net scene, but was so light on his feet that he actually danced on water, albeit, for a very short time.

Fishing lies are not only fun; they provide opportunity for great repartee. For instance, if you tell me that you caught a female octopus in Green Lake, I'll tell you about the time I reeled in a perfectly good lantern while night-fishing on Oneida.

"Well," you'll say, "the *really* amazing thing was I could tell it was a *female* octopus because it was wearing *silk panties!*"

To which I would reply, "Wow, that's really something—did I mention the lantern was *still lit when I fished it out?*"

Yup, a true fisherman, that's me!

4. Tell 'em What They Wanna Hear

*H*erewith, *a meditation in three acts, concerning the finer points of interpersonal communication.*

1. Caught in No-Man's Land

Umpteen years ago, when I was courting my first wife, I made the mistake of going through the "gotcha!" section of Liverpool with my mind on my manhood instead of the speedometer.

You see, back in those ancient days, everyone knew Catholic girls didn't do it at all before they got married, and Jewish girls were known for not doing it at all *after* they got married. Everyone was wrong, but that's what everyone knew. Back then, you might make-out with a girl, which meant playing kissy face—not what it means today—but any attempts at making-out—as it is meant today—were met with slaps, tears and stern warnings—slaps, tears and stern warnings very much like the ones I just got from my own fair maiden.

Now you understand why I was distracted as I went through that stretch of open road that starts the Onondaga Lake Parkway, but still carries the township speed limit. But it isn't really a No-Man's Land; no, no. As many of us have found out, it's more like Da Man's Land.

There I was, driving along on a four-lane highway and wishing they'd hurry up and invent stretch pants, when a red bubble-gum machine pulled alongside.

Officer Unfriendly motioned me to pull over.

"Where do you work, Son?" (I thought they were supposed to say "license and registration" first.)

"I sell Cutco Cutlery, Sir."

I want you to know, Dear Reader, that I was not selling mere knives, no sir! I was selling the finest cutlery ever honed. "This product, madam, is not guaranteed for ten years, it is not guaranteed for life, it is, believe it or not—and I want you to listen very carefully to what I'm going to say next—it is guaranteed *forever*. Yes, Ma'am, I did say *for-e-ver*. Should anything ever happen to these knives—and of course it never will—but hypothetically, if it did, you—and not just you, not just your children, but even your great-*grandchildren*—would be able to get them replaced absolutely free, *F-R-E-E*, free. If you take a look at that handle, you'll start to understand why. That's ebonite you're looking at—the same stuff they make bowling balls out of. Just look at the way..."

But wait a sec, why did he ask me where I worked instead of asking for my license and registration? Then in a flash it came to me. Liverpool was a General Electric town—a company town—and cops tend to be pro-union. Quickly I added, "Yeah, I gotta sell this stuff until the strike is settled at G.E."

He let me go with a verbal warning.

2. I'll Fight Ya With Both Hands Tied Behind My Back

"You boys were in a fight last night, weren't you?" Phil's mother asked.

"No, honest, we weren't, Mom," Phil said.

"What kind of a fool do you take me for? Art has a black eye, and I can see the scabs from fist marks on his face. No wonder he slept over here; he probably didn't dare go home looking like that."

I tried to explain: "We were on our way here from the dance. Phil was on the sidewalk and I cut across the church lawn. You know how it slopes down a little there? Well, I didn't realize it was all ice, and I fell and banged my eye—and every time I tried to get up, I would slip again and that's how I got all the cuts."

It was hopeless. She wasn't going to believe us, even though that was exactly the way it happened.

We went to my house so I could change clothes—hoping I could do so before anyone else saw me. But my luck was no good: my mother was on the back porch, hanging clothes. (For you younger readers, clothes wet from washing were clipped outdoors to a rope, using clothespins. The rope itself was on pulleys and — oh, never mind!) There was to be no quick and easy, sneaking in and out for me.

"What *happened* to you?" my mother shouted.

Well, I wasn't about to tell the truth again!

"I learned that I should keep my mouth shut when I'm around guys tougher than me."

"Okay, Son," she said with a sigh. "I'll let it slide because you didn't try to lie to me."

3. The Empty Nest Gambit

"License and Registration!" (See? I knew they were supposed to start there!)

"Whassa prollem officer?"

"You crossed the center line twice."

"Yeh, the power steerin' on this car is very touchy. 'S like driving a sponge upshtream..."

"That could be, but I suspect you have been drinking, Mr. Belge, and I'm afraid I'm going to have to give you..."

"Yer darn tootin', I been drinkin'! You've got my regish..my resha..my ID, so you know how ol' I am. I got *sev'n childern* and the younges' one is fin'ly gonna grada...grazsh...she's a senior in high school. I'm thinkin' of a little relief 'n life, a few things for me 'n the wife—shit, maybe even some fishin' now 'n then. 'N this mornin', my wife, who's fourteen years younger'n me, she tells me she's *preggant* and no way is she gonna have a 'bortion! Don' gemme wrong, I love alla my kids fiercely. But it's like I jush got outta prisz...prizm...jail,'n now the warden's saying 'Nother twenny years, fella!'

"So, yeah, I admit it, Ossifer. We had a big fight 'n I said some shit and wen' out drinkin' an' I just stopped 'n I was goin' home t'polo...polio...say 'sorry' when you pulled me over."

"Hey look, you've got a tough problem, but I can't let you drive," he said. "I'll follow you to that diner just a few feet up the road. Call somebody to come get you and have some coffee—and good luck."

Once I got home, I had to shake Starr several times to wake her. "Honey, anybody call?"

"No, why?"

"I tol' 'em yer preggant."

"I'm what?"

"Umm, I, I, I tol' 'em yer pretty."

"Oh, go to sleep, you old sot."

Successful communication: Just tell 'em what they wanna hear.

5. Answering the Call

In many a young man's life there is a neighborhood bar that he and his friends hang out in. And in each of these local watering holes, there is always one character who has a story worth telling.

This is Ricky's story.

The first thing you need to know about Ricky is that he was not too bright—a fact he proved, time after time. He was famous for fractured expressions like "in one head and out the other," and "I can read you like the back of my hand," and "if you don't know...don't ask." He always claimed to be "lactate intolerable," which disappointed none of the ladies, for sure, or as he would have put it, "There's no two doubts about *that*."

No, Ricky was not the most vibrant crayon in the box. As a matter of fact, I think his intellectual palette consisted of black, white and—on a good day—gray.

As it turned out, this was a good day.

There Ricky sat with his head on the bar, passed out as usual, when the pay-phone rang.

Now, there's a protocol to answering such calls in a bar full of delinquent men. If you don't want to lie, don't answer the phone. Because if you do, you may end up speaking to an irate wife demanding to know in bitter tones if her husband is there. Answering "yes" may salve your soul, but it may create a need for salving your body as well, because the husband may not appreciate you telling his wife he's at the bar. No, your job is to let wifey hear you call out hubby's name. If his response is a frantic waving of his hands while shaking his head "no" but you say "yes," your honesty will get you into a bit of a jam, or a pickle, or some other troublesome, preserved foodstuff.

However, if you are a fibber like me, McGee, no sweat! You simply hold out the phone, look right at the man, and call his name. Then you say, "No ma'am, I'm sorry but he's not here."

You assure her that, if he does show up, you'll have him call her right away. And you hang up.

In this particular case, when the phone rang, a fibber (me) answered the call. I paused according to protocol, then loudly called Ricky's name.

Ricky, it turns out, was surprisingly less *non compos mentis* than his previous *modus operandus* might suggest; peeling his face from the bar, he delivered the most sage advice I've ever heard:

"Aw, jus' tell 'er what she wants t' hear."

Everyone in the place roared with laughter. It was the perfect response. Meanwhile Ricky's head fell back to the bar with a thunk.

"No, ma'am," I fibbed, stifling a laugh. "Ricky's not here.... Yes, I certainly will."

For years to come, every time the phone rang in that bar it was met with a raucous chorus of "Tell 'er what she wants to hear!" Followed by gales of well-lubricated laughter.

6. Camp Everest

*F*or thirty-six years I dabbled at running a restaurant. Eventually, I decided it just wasn't a success and sold it. It was built around a devotion to good food, a menu filled with wacky dinner names, signs based on humor, a menu loaded with double entendres, and a fun-loving staff.

Every summer we closed down for two weeks regeneration. One year, I rented a camp and after swilling a few too many, invited my staff, customers and friends to join us. Following is an honest-to-God-all-these-things-actually-happened accounting of the weekend.

Mary is quite a funny gal. Actually she's a *quiet* funny gal, so quiet that you have to listen carefully, lest you miss some real comic gold.

Her first comment upon arrival was, "We started out with two cars. I think we lost one—the one with the lawyer in it. Do we get a prize?"

The second person out of the car was Donald. He took one look at the thirty-foot embankment between the camp and the lake and immediately dubbed it *Camp Everest*. With just those two words, he painted a caricature that would have taken Paul Harvey fifteen minutes to describe—five minutes without...his... dramatic...pauses.

To give you a further example of Donald's wit, at one point during this weekend, our cook, Ron, mentioned that in his youth one of his big toes had turned green. Fearing gangrene, although he could remember no trauma to that foot, he went to a podiatrist. The doctor had no idea of the cause, but eventually Ron's toe returned to normal on its own. Donald looked up from his book and wryly commented, "Stupid doctor; couldn't even diagnose main toe poisoning."

A couple of years earlier, Donald visited us at our camp on

Hatch Lake and swore that he had been chased by a sea monster while swimming. He also has an imagination that, when fueled by gin, takes left turns faster and more often than Al Unser. He called it "The Hatch Ness Monster," nicknamed it Hatchie, and cautioned all newcomers to beware. His antics over the next few days—capped by a 3:00 am attempt to swim the lake, underwater and naked—brought us to realize who or what Hatchie really was. This year, he swore that Hatchie had migrated to Camp Everest and everyone was in danger—of that we had no doubt.

The first two people out of the second car were Crystal and Harvey-the-Lawyer. (Yes, they did find us, so I was forced to take back Mary's prize, although she had already drunk it—although "drunken it" would be more apropos.) These two madcaps raced down to the end of the dock, where Crystal threw a block worthy of Alex Karras into Harvey, dumping him into the lake. It fell to all of us whenever swimming thereafter to search the muck for Harvey's keys, which were lost in what became known as "Crystal's Harvey Cream."

Great gamesmen, we; we pursued the trivial that first night until 4:00 am. Poor Crystal never got one answer right. I mean never, nada, zilch, zero, none. But then the laws of probability do not favor someone who answers the question, "What communicable childhood disease is most responsible for infant deaths?" with an immediate, "Only one thing fits that—VD!" Donald immediately shouted, "You got that right, bitch!"—a screaming epithet which he consequently used to label her every answer.

Finally, at 4:00 am, he gleefully cried for the millionth time, "You got that right, bitch! Your team wins. The game is over!" You must realize how much we all wanted to go to bed, since he got no argument from anyone, even though her answer, "Transvestites," was in response to the question, "What makes Drambuie sweet?"

On Saturday, a bunch of us decided to take a three-mile boat trip to the islands. I was driving the motorboat and towing the canoe, which was occupied by Harvey, Ron, and Starr. About a quarter of the way there, we ran out of gas.

"There's a marina a little way up," I pointed out. "You guys in the canoe can row there and back in no time. Meanwhile, we'll row as far as *we* can to meet you."

Now, I should stop our story's progress to explain some things to you. Firstly, the marina was not a short distance—it was close to two miles away. Secondly, while we had already covered a mile, most of it was in circumnavigating a peninsula. So we could have rowed to shore, walked an eighth of a mile to our car, and gone for gas. Thirdly, with my well-publicized bad back, *I* wasn't going to be doing the rowing. Fourthly, I was going to be in the back facing the passengers doing the rowing. Filthily, my passengers were Belinda, Cerise, Mary and Crystal, four lovely ladies in bathing suits upon whom God had graciously bestowed his abundance. I sure wasn't about to mutiny that bounty. And sexily, the cold beer was in our boat.

I did make one mistake: I appointed Belinda coxswain. I didn't know that she went out in the canoe with Crystal the night before and panicked worse than Teddy Kennedy at Chappaquiddick. Her hands, they tell me, clenched the sides of the canoe tighter than Mae West's bodice clenched her bosom, her face a Mia Farrow white. As coxswain, she was sitting in the front facing the prow with whichever of the other women was taking a break from rowing. The two who were rowing were in the center seat facing me, sitting astern (drool, drool, slobber, slobber). When the coxswain wanted the boat to go to her left, she had to call "right oar."

She never mastered the reversal.

"Right oar!" she would call.

"Right *oar!*" she would holler.

"Right *OOOAARR!*" she would scream.

"Oops! I mean *left* oar," she would mutter.

Circle by circle we made our way down the lake, rowing one mile to accomplish a quarter mile. We didn't care. We were singing, drinking beer, laughing, getting sunshine, fresh air, each in his or her own way enjoying the bouncing waves.

About halfway to the marina, Mary exclaimed, "I can swim faster than you guys can row." With that, she jumped overboard and started swimming—about three strokes—and came up laughing, saying, "Shit! I could *walk* it faster than you guys could row," and stood up in the knee-deep water.

When we got to the island, Starr was very upset. I assumed it was over my role as King Leer, but not so; her *casus belli* was far more justifiable: we had drunk all the beer. To masticate an old political slogan, "Not tipsy in the canoe, they were ticked off, too."

Saturday night went pretty much like the night before. Everybody played games, drank and laughed. But this time it was Melissa's turn to be the center of attention. Normally, Melissa was sweet and demure. She never spoke loudly or acted unladylike. She was the epitome of the propriety that every father wants his daughter to become and his son to marry.

That is, until she gets into the vodka. Then, Miss Prissy sheds her primrose propriety faster than Little Egypt stripping off her g-string and becomes...*Slut-girl!*

Slut-girl left no breast unbared in her quest to win the Mary Magdalene Cup. She was loud and lewd. When our landlady stopped in for a friendly visit, we had to gag Melissa to keep her from cussing the poor lady out. Once the landlady had gone, Melissa's retort to our having restrained her was eloquent, succinct and direct.

She mooned us.

Thus ends the tale of Camp Everest. Next year, I think we'll go to the Marianas Trench just to see what new lows we can plumb.

7. Going to the Faire

Big Whitey is my buddy. Looking for me? Find Big Whitey, and there I'll be. Well, that's how it used to be; but after the way I misused him this past weekend, he may not want to be close to me for quite a while.

Big Whitey is my truck—a big, white, windowless, two-ton delivery truck.

Several weeks ago, a bunch of us were guzzling the grape in Arturo's tavern and reminiscing about my son, Bart. After a sabbatical of several years, Bart would again be sheriff at the Sterling Renaissance Faire that season. His quick wit (he is *my* son!) at the Ducking Pond and the Wench Auction—and ad-libbing as he strolled the grounds in character—made him such an attraction that the managerial staff welcomed his return.

The Arturo's crew used to make an annual hegira to see him, as well as several other cast members who were also friends and/or customers. We always had such a good time that, this night, we decided that the Renaissance trip should be given a renaissance.

Do you remember the misadventures of this maniacal group at Camp Everest a couple of years ago? And do you remember me saying that the saga would continue?

The saga continues.

Before we set out for the faire, Ron (of "main toe poisoning" infamy) had a clever idea. In order to get a bit of air circulation in the back of Big Whitey, he devised a way to partially open the over-dead whore.

Maybe I better explain that. You see, a while back, Cherise, in an honest *lapsis lingua*—I know ye of little faith thought I didn't learn anything from three years of Latin under the black bears at Saint Paul, but fie on you because, *ipso facto*, I did. Anyway, Cherise once called Big Whitey's overhead door by that name, and so it has been called by Arturians ever since. Reverend Spooner has nothing on us!

In order to rig the over-dead whore so she would stay partially open and provide the passengers therein a modicum of breathable air, I offered Ron a two-by-four, which he promptly discarded, and a three-hundred-foot rope which he used in its entirety. A mere forty-five minutes later he had ropes running in fifteen directions. There were ropes to hold the door open, and ropes to hold the door closed. There were ropes to counteract those ropes, and ropes tying all of the crisscrossing ropes together. The whole arachnid array looked like a Rube Goldberg demonstration of Archimedes principle, but, somehow, it worked.

We shoved a cooler full of beer and booze in Big Whitey's back end (he never seemed to mind), stuck in some chairs, cushions and a cot, and we were off in style—and in our heads.

I drove Big Whitey and the human contents of his bowels to the Faire. Accompanying me in the cab was a new addition to our crew, Porky.

"Porky," I said. "You'll notice the signs at intersections pointing to the Faire. There are no signs, however, on the way back pointing to home. Since everyone but Ron will be schnockered when we leave, there will be a unanimous appeal to have him replace me as the desiccated diver. But since he's riding in the back and can't see the turns we take, it's anybody's guess where we'll end up tonight. So I want you to try to remember how we got here, okay?

"And another thing, I'm doing my best to take it easy on the folks in back—taking it easy on the curves, trying not to jam on the brakes, etc. But Ron is in the back and doesn't realize that— he's under the delusion that I'm driving normally. So, on the way back, he'll drive in *his* normal manner. I'm not saying he's reckless—but he is. So he's sure to provide his human cargo with a roller-coaster-y thrill."

Porky just nodded and went back to cleaning his gun.

When you enter the Renaissance Faire, your first reaction is that this is not an Olde English Festival; this is a carnivore's convention. Everyone has a giant turkey leg going from their paw to their maw. I don't mean to sound like a purist—or a Puritan—but you'll also see baked potatoes, corn on the cob, and tobacco, all of which, like the turkey, came from the "New World"—*not* Elizabethan England. And I really cannot accept ice cream as Renaissance. Oh, I know they had something like it—but it was fish flavored more often than not and excuse me while I barf.

Well, it didn't take two seconds for Ron and Porky to get into their customary food frenzy. Those two will eat anything that moos...or doesn't. They classify matter into animal, vegetable or inedible. It's been rumored that their ancestors were responsible for the disappearance of Atlantis, having eaten so much they sank it. If these two had been born girls, they could have been porn stars—everything they get their hands on goes straight into their mouths. For instance, at the Festival of Nations Exhibit at the New York State Fair, Ron ate something from every one of the dozens of stands...and then went back for more from the ones he liked best. He earned my amazement—and my envy, because I knew he wouldn't gain an ounce.

One improvement I noticed at the Faire was the increase in outhouses—or *privies* as the *rennies* refer to them. They weren't so plentiful a decade ago, when I was chased after by one of those rennies. To his credit, he never broke character as he hollered, "Sire, thou shalt not pisseth in yon apple orchard!"

At the end of the day, Ron drove us a few miles to an area of Lake Ontario called The Bluffs. National Geographic once rated the sunsets at The Bluffs to be second best in the world. Someplace in Japan, the Land of the Rising Sun, took first. Go figger. The road going to The Bluffs, however, has earned no such distinctions. It is so bad, it makes the first mile of the old Golf Road in Mycenae look like the Lincoln Highway. If you've never been up the old Golf Road, by all means try it. It twists and turns and climbs so straightly vertically up that you fear you'll be met at the top by Thor, waiting for you with a lightning bolt in each hand. "Hold, Dweebleshite! Just back it right down where you came from, and I mean now!" Try imagining all of that, along with ruts, rubble and no pavement, and you've got the Bluff Road.

Ron, true to form, drove the Bluff Road at his normal speed eliciting such shrieks, screams and curses from Big Whitey's rear end that incredulous bystanders figured he was transporting new residents to Dante's Inferno.

The trip home was not without benefit, however; Ron learned that you don't use the emergency brake in a strange vehicle. You may remember the *Reader's Digest* article, "I Am Your Emergency Brake: Use Me or Lose Me." The first—and, so far as I know, the only—rule regarding emergency brakes is: *Always* use them, or *never* use them. Because once you stop using them, they rust and seize up.

Ron obviously always used his, and I, conversely, never used mine. Ten miles down the road, on the outskirts of Oswego, the shrieks of the other passengers in the back coalesced into "Smoke! Smoke!"

"No thanks," I hollered from the passenger seat, "gave it up years ago."

After Starr quite sensibly used her half-eaten turkey leg to beat against the wall of the cab, they got their point across. We stopped by the side of the road and took turns crawling under Big Whitey and beating on his brake drum with rocks, pipes, whatever was at hand until we freed him from the clutch of the Iron Maiden's rusted fist. Thereafter, we thoughtfully made regular stops along the way to give the brakes time to cool down and to let someone—and every third block, there was a someone—out to take a leak.

Sorry, Big Whitey, I promise to treat you better in the future. And this time I mean it. No bluffing.

8. Jock Itch

Several years ago, my best friends, Rum and Dumb, told me they had come across a boat for sale. It came with a trailer and a fine running outboard motor. They knew it was fine running, because, not being country bumpkins, they'd demanded that the seller give them a trial run. Also, being two of the sharpest hagglers this side of Shylock, they had dickered the seller down to half his original asking price.

A little sanding, a coat of paint, a couple hundred apiece, and we three would be ruling the Great Briny.

"How about it, want in?"

"Sure!"

Oh what grief I did engender, with that short and simple answer.

We dubbed ourselves the World's Worst Yachtsmen (WWY) and set to work. For several weeks we scraped, sanded and screwed; planed, primed and painted. Finally, it was seaworthy. All we needed now were a few common supplies—oil, spark plugs, beer, shear pins, beer, those sorts of things. Lay those in, and the *Jock Itch* would be ready for launching.

It was in the attempt to get these supplies that we glimpsed a glimmer of the foul weather ahead. We landlubbers were about to learn that God was *not* in his heaven and all was *not* right with the world. In short, Rum was unable to find the most common-ly-stocked spare part for any engine, the sheer pin. Eventually we found out why: the Scott Engine Company had gone out of business twenty years before.

With roe on our faces and our rudders tucked between our mizzenmasts, we called the man who sold us the boat and asked him where he had taken the engine for repairs. He gave us the address of a man up near Cicero, who turned out to be the last Scott engine repairman in Central New York, perhaps the world.

This we learned from the repairman's wife. She went on to tell us, rather proudly and with a little tear in her eye, that he was eighty-eight years old—*when he passed away late last fall*. Hmm, the guy who sold us the boat must have forgotten to mention that fact.

We had sailed willy-nilly into our very own Bermuda triangle, but we would find a way out. We were not giver-uppers. Somewhere, someone had to repair those damn motors and we would find him. After all, we were following in the oar-strokes of our intrepid seafaring forersailors. *Columbus* didn't quit. The *Argonauts* didn't quit. *Anna Edson Taylor* didn't quit. Of course, we were only over a figurative barrel; she was in a literal barrel, the first one over Niagara Falls—which was where we seemed to be heading, as well. But only figuratively, not literally, of course, that would be silly. We all wouldn't fit in a barrel.

Well, shiver me timbers! We finally found our repairman—and one much younger and alive-er than the deceased super-octogenarian in Cicero. This one was only seventy, and if you discounted his several heart attacks, in very good health.

He got *Jock Itch* up and running, thank God. We put out to sea. I know, I should have said "put out to lake," but that lacks a certain dramatic flair.

Rum, who already had the heebie-jeebies about being swallowed by sea monsters (I know, I know, *lake* monsters), or being spewed about by giant waterspouts and being marooned on a desert island, now added a new fear to his repertoire, to wit: reading the *Syracuse Herald Urinal* and finding our new repairman in the obits. You will note that nightmares are noted for tacking around logic, as this one certainly did. I mean, why would our local paper publish an obit for a man who lived in Watertown, seventy-five nautical miles away as the flying fish flew? I tried to impress this upon Rum, but he just rolled over in his berth and went back to counting sharks.

All of this should have served as ominous omens that no savvy sailor would ignore.

We ignored them all.

Not three minutes into our maiden voyage, Dumb got confused ("...but only for a second!") about which lever was the forward picker-upper and which was the reverse slow-er-downer—and that's how *Jock Itch* lost most of her newly refurbished aluminum railings to an almost-high-enough dock.

Heartbroken over marring our *flor-del-mar*, we returned to camp.

Besides, we were out of beer.

Any old salt worth his, will tell you that such incidents were Neptune's revenge; we had ignored his warnings, and smashing *Jock Itch's* superficial superstructure was just his first cast, so to speak.

Next, he attacked the engine, simultaneously spearing all three forward speeds on his trident. It was castration on the high seas.

Next, thank you very much, he sent in his buddy, St. Elmo. Ignoring our pleas for mercy, Elmo entombed us in dense, dark storm clouds and lobbed the occasional ball of lightning at us, robbing us of all sense of direction—cleaving us from the very bosom of our fellow man.

Lastly, he brewed up a foul Sou'wester and laughed as we three drunks struggled to navigate the tricky channel at the mouth of the Little Salmon River—a channel flanked by boulders only slightly less massive than Muhammad Ali's ego—in a storm on a lake known for swallowing bigger fish than we—in a dinghy with no forward gears.

Fortunately, a real seaman was on shore and saw us floundering. He came out in his boat and in spite of our attempts to assist him, towed us to port. It really was a clever feat of seamanship. So much so, that after failing to convince our savior to exercise his right of salvage, we tried to hire him on as Captain Jock Itch. As grateful as he was for this exciting opportunity, he had to decline our offer. His actual response was something like, "I'd rather have the Albatross, thank you!" The deal would have fallen through anyway, when we found out that not only did he not drink, but being only ten, he had to be home by dusk.

Once again we made the overland trek to Watertown for repairs. Any prudent man would, at this point, realize that this boat was getting more mileage by land than by sea, and maybe it was time to unload this Good Ship Lolli-Plop on some other poor sucker.

But the WWY are not prudent men, thus the foregoing incident was followed by a deluge of similarly losing experiences.

We lost the channel leading to camp.

We lost water skiers in the dark.

We lost water skis in broad daylight. (Has anyone ever seen narrow daylight?)

We lost the bilge drain plug over the side, and rode around until we were almost out of gas, trying to figure out how to stop without sinking. Rum and Dumb finally agreed to Rum's suggestion to get it close to shore, cut the engine, and use the boat-trailer crank and brute force to wrestle her in.

We lost the prop, and then we almost lost me, because I insisted that I could reattach it while the waves slammed me rhythmically from side to side against the insides of the boat. I felt like the clapper of Quasimodo's bell, but attach it I did. You can't beat this German for stubbornness.

Our final attempt to put the *Jock Itch* and the WWY securely into Davy Jones Locker occurred after a long day of fishing, beer-guzzling, and girl-gawking. It was early evening when the terrible trio decided to get gas, more beer, and make the trip from the Little Salmon River across Ontario Lake to the Oswego Harbor. I remember thinking this a superbly stout idea, but since I'd passed out shortly after the decision was made, I remember nothing else until I woke up in a stalled boat somewhere in the middle of Lake Ontario.

"Whassa prollem?" I slobbered.

"Outta gas," Rum answered.

"But di'n we stop t'get some?"

"Yeh," said Dumb, "but the las' open marina's outta gas."

"Well, did you ask him if we could make it to Oswego with what we had?"

"Uh huh, he said, 'no effin' way'."

Rum kept trying to start the engine. I begged him to stop. We were too far off the American shore to swim and the wind was blowing us steadily toward Canada. It was my thinking that we ought to save the battery for sending SOS signals. But, then again, we hadn't seen another boat since sunset.

Rum said he heard a gurgling from the tank and thought if we could get it started, drove slowly and kept on an even keel, we might get some more distance.

Lo and behold, hearken, hail and hallelujah—the engine started!

Of course, we took the shortest course to salvation and headed straight for shore. Not because that was the smart thing to do—that was just a side benefit. We had set out to get beer, and beer we would get.

After a couple of leagues—or was it fathoms? All I really knew was we were in deep—we saw the modern-day equivalent of a lighthouse—the neon Sirens of commerce winking enticingly from shore. When the boat was finally tied up to the dock, the onlookers wanted to know how the WWY had done the almost impossible.

"You mean, get here from the Little Salmon without enough beer?" Rum asked. "How'd you know about that?"

"No! The rocks! The rocks!" a shore dweller answered. "Even in narrow daylight, boats that try to land here get smashed up. Didn't you see the rocks?"

"No," I answered. "All we saw was the Budweiser sign."

After warming our outsides up and cooling our insides down, we flipped coins, and it became my duty to find gas. It cost me a drink to bribe the cook into giving me two large plastic containers. It cost me five dollars to bribe a patron into driving me to town to get gas. Getting a gas station attendant to forget there was a plastic container law was more expensive; that cost me twenty. We had apparently landed on the Bribery Coast.

After refueling ourselves and *Jock Itch*, we took on provisions—several six-packs—for the return trip. The bar emptied to watch the ship of fools try to retrace its path through the Gates of Hades.

Somehow, we made it.

We sold *Jock Itch* the next spring.

9. Mama Told Me Not to Come

I can't believe it!

The crowd is booing. The game hasn't even started yet and the crowd is actually booing. Catch this—they aren't booing a ref or an ump or even anyone on the field, because there *is* no one on the field. They're booing the announcement naming the players on the opposing team. This is a sport? These are sports fans? What-in-hell, I wonder, has become of sportsmanship?

When the opponents actually did take the field—well actually, they didn't take a field, they took a huge, green outdoor carpet painted with stripes, numbers and logos but that's another topic, altogether—the boos and raspberries became a roar.

Shades of Sister Mary Malicious save us! When I went to school, the nuns taught us to show courtesy to visitors. You knew they were visitors and not black knights carrying buckets of bubonic plague, because right up on the scoreboard it said, "Visitors" on one side, and "Home Team" on the other.

You are their host. You do not boo your guests. I mean, *it just isn't done.*

Can you envision sitting down at a card table in someone's home, and before the cards are dealt the host and hostess start booing you? Or Alex Trebek saying, "As soon as our audience stops booing the newcomers, we'll get to work."?

I was very tempted to raise my hands at the end of the game, and in my sternest school teacher's voice say, "All right, people, sit right back down. Not one of you is leaving until you've all written 'I will not be rude to guests' on the scoreboard one hundred times."

What the fans are doing may be viewed as simply an extension of the game itself; a game where many players do whatever they can do, legal or ill, so long as they think they have a decent chance to get away with their indecencies. If they can mask, grab, or slip in a clip, they're going to. Of course, throwing dirt in an opponent's eyes is a lot more difficult with AstroTurf.

At pro games guards with vicious dogs patrol the perimeter to stop fans from rushing the field at the end of the game. Attack dogs? Really? My Lordy, what kind of people are we?

At the end of the bloodbath, figuratively and literally, on the field and off, I scanned the stands, but no emperor sat imperiously enthroned above the Romanesque rabble as I had half expected. He was probably at home nursing his carpal thumbnail syndrome, brought on from all that ix-naying.

So no one got thrown to the lions or tossed into a fiery pit, this time.

Next time I come to this stadium, I'm bringing dog biscuits and a nice, big, soup bone. Not for the attack dogs, for the crowd.

On second thought, that ain't no way to have fun, son. Next time I come to the stadium, *I'm staying home.*

10. On Being Physically Pffft

few years or more back, *A Dud at 70, a Stud at 80*, by Noel
Johnson hit the Best Seller's list. I loved that title! And it had
special import to me, because at that time I was exactly sixty years
old, and physically a dud. If I was this bad now, imagine how
much worserer off I would be in ten years!

I never bothered to read the book, but the title made it clear
that change was possible—and if I was honest with the man in the
mirror, change was highly warranted. I'd dedicated my life to sins
of the flesh, and let my musculature degenerate into Jello.

I decided to get reacquainted with my inner stud.

Just prior to not reading *At 70* (and if there ever was a book
worth not reading, this was it) I read one of the Travis McGee
books by John D. MacDonald. I've always been impressed by
MacDonald's range of subject matter, and by the astuteness of his
observations. Yes, I am very impressionable, always have been. I
think my impressionablism started developing at about the same
time my younger older brother started hitting me upside the head.
That always left an impression. Anyway, one of the posits in one
of his books was that many people who decide to become physically fit take up running when they can't even walk from here to
the corner without stopping for a rest. How in hell do they think
they can run three miles if they can't walk three feet? They doom
themselves to frustration and failure before their first step.

Not me! I would start out walking. When I could walk three
miles without pain, then—and only then—would I start to run.
I mean, running is healthful exercise, but not if you drop dead
while you doing it.

I've been walking four to six days a week for almost three
years. When I first started, I could only walk about two miles at a
stretch. I'm up to about three kilometers now, and before the year
is out, I truly believe I'll be covering ten thousand feet a day.

In spite of this excellent record of improvement, I still have some pain in my legs when I walk, so running is going to have to wait for another couple of years—or at least until I'm up to three thousand yards a day. Strangely, my left leg hurts more than my right, despite the fact that I'm pretty consistent about using them both when I'm walking. Now, when I'm *driving*, I use my right leg a lot more. Is this causing my left leg to atrophy? Maybe I'm wasting time with all this walking, when the cure may be as simple as driving a British car.

I really am proud of the fact that I was able to avoid some of the errors others have made. Take aerobics, for example. Who wants to do an exercise that no one can spell? Besides, I think all that jumping up and down may be causing some of the problems that older people have with their kidneys.

And other forms of exercise, although they may be easier to spell, pose their own dangers: there's tennis elbow, bicycle knee, punch drunkenness and God knows what-all.

Did you know that weight lifters have the shortest life spans of all athletes?

So I guess I'll just stick to my new regimen, which I'll be promoting in my new book, *Drive Yourself to Better Health*. Not that I'm really writing a whole book. As Mr. Johnson and I have already proven, a snappy title is all you need.

11. Fishing without a License

A car goes by and I cringe; it happens every single time. I'm doing my best to act nonchalant, just in case one of those cars whizzing by carries a game warden. I figure if I act real casual, like I'm in my own neighborhood, the game warden will assume that I have a license.

At least that's what the left side of my brain is saying. The part of my brain that hasn't left is telling me that Vanna White's impression of John Wayne has a better chance of winning an Oscar than my impersonation of an innocent man.

So here I am, fishing on the causeway, doing my best not to look any more awkward than Frankenstein's monster would if he were walking on stilts. And while I'm fishing, I'm cursing the governor of this fine State. "You've raised the ^$%*=* license fee another three @!$%^# bucks! You've raised everything *up, up, up.* The only thing you haven't raised is our opinion of you! I always agreed with your stand against capital punishment, but taxes this &^$%#@ high ought to be a capital *%$&#- offense!

I'm in this sorry plight (is there such a thing as an un-sorry plight?) because, although fishing licenses are still required by law (for more and more bread), nobody sells the damn things no more, not no one, not no how, not no where; not in sports shops; not in bait shops and definitely not at the game warden's office, wherever that is. In the old days, the good old days, a sportsman got up at five o'clock in the morning, went to a bait shop, bought bait and a fishing license and went and got a fish.

Not nowadays! Now, you've got to go downtown to some high-rise State office building to get one—a license, not a fish. And let me ask you, do you think they're going to be open at five of the clock in the ante meridian? Ain't no gub'ment folk I ever heard of up and about at that hour, 'ceptin' those on Gary Hart's boat or in Teddy Kennedy's car, but we'll cross those bridges after we've burned them.

Suffice it to say, it has become so unprofitable to sell fishing licenses that even Sears doesn't sell them anymore. You remember Sears, the "If we don't carry it, it doesn't exist" store? Well, they don't carry fishing licenses, so what does that tell you?

So there I am, cringing licenseless on the causeway, and I get to thinking about this story that a fisherman friend swore was true—which is my only reason for doubting it:

Once upon a day, a game warden approaches my friend and his fishing buddy and asks to see their licenses. My friend drops his pole and takes off like you might if Tammy Bakker was eying your crotch. After a quarter of a mile or so, the warden catches up to him, which made him fast as well as game, and starts to write up my buddy's buddy for fishing without a license.

"But, Sir," my friend informs him, "I have a fishing license!"

"Then why did you run?"

Excuse me for interrupting myself, but that reminds me of another story. Two hunters are being chased by this humongous bear, when one guy turns to the other and asks if there's a chance they can outrun the bear.

"It doesn't really matter," the first hunter says.

"What do you mean, it doesn't matter?" The second hunter demands.

Excuse me for interrupting myself yet again, but that reminds me of yet another story: A hunter once told me of the time he and a wolf shared a ledge that ran along the face of a steep cliff. No way up, and no way down. His rifle jammed, so he waved it in the wolf's face as he backed up. What small advantage he might have had was quickly disappearing as he slipped and slid with every backward step.

"Weren't you scared?" I asked.

Return with me now, as the castaway on the causeway does his best to appear at ease.

A car is slowing down and my stomach feels like it's being walloped from the inside by Cassius Clay. Damn, it's a game warden. Act cool. Give him a little wave. Double damn. He's stopping.

The warden strolls out onto the causeway with a smile like he's thinking, "It's so worth a little walk to see the how-the-hell-did-you-know-I-don't-have-a-license look on your face!"

And I'm thinking, "I don't have a buddy with a license to distract him, and I definitely can't outrun him—oh, God, I just might shit myself!"

But, a man has his pride, you know. I went quietly. No shit.

12. Professional Sport

I'm writing this on SB Sunday, which all jocks know stands for "Super Bowl."

I am not a jock. I am, in fact, a sports dunce—something the patrons of Arturo's don't know about me. They sit next to me at the bar and say, "Who do you think will win the game tomorrow?" They don't really give a pile of nitrogenous waste what my opinion is; they just want some friendly conversation. And I want to stay in this particular closet, so I can't admit that I don't have a clue. In fact, I don't even know which teams are playing. In fact, in fact, in most cases I'm not even sure what sport is being played. So my answer is usually in the form of a question like, "What point spread are the bookies giving?" If they say, "Dallas is getting seven," I say, "Really? Hmm. Does that seem right to you?" Now we've got a conversation going, which makes them happy, without my letting on how little I know, which makes me happy.

When I left the bar last evening, I said, "Happy Super Bowl Sunday Eve, everyone!" They all giggled, but it's not too far from the truth. I mean, as a national holiday, it doesn't rank up there with Christmas and Easter, but it crushes the heart out of Valentine's Day and makes kindling of Arbor Day.

Last night I was making the chart for our SB numbers pool, we were gambling just for fun, Officer Friendly, honest, and I realized I only knew one of the teams playing, so I slyly asked, "The home team goes across the top, who's that again?" Someone said, "The Bills." Well, dammit, that was the team I already knew. So I had to leave the place for the other team's name blank while I made busy work, 'til someone piped up, "You gonna put the Cowboys in?"

"I didn't think there'd be any Dallas fans this far north, but if you insist..."

Professional sports are not the only man-centric things I'm not attuned to. I'm confused about the declension of military ranks—the ranks of the ranks, as it were. I'm pretty sure a general and an admiral have reached their zeniths, on land and at sea. But, other than that...

And when the War-to-Start-Up-All-Wars-Again was a-waging, I couldn't tell one airplane from another. "That was a P52," one of the guys would say, and I'd reply, "Yup, it sure was." I think I was actually afraid to learn the planes, because then I would know when the German bombers were here. Knowing what they looked like seemed like one step closer to seeing them—maybe even causing them to appear.

Marvelous Marvin sounds like a wrestler to me, but I think he's actually a boxer. Even so, I wouldn't put any money on him because I never watch either sport. As far as I'm concerned they're only slightly less pugilistic than ice hockey, and ten times as boring. But if you want to be bored—truly bored—go to a tractor-pull. It's an hour and a huff of huffing in diesel fumes and dust, and having your ear drums drummed until they bleed, followed by fifteen seconds of metal-on-metal mayhem.

Guys are supposed to like stuff like that?

It's not that I'm a couch potato—I'm more of a barstool banana. I get my exercise hefting a pool cue, and for competition—well, that's why God invented the drinking game.

Now, *there's* a sport any man can relate to.

13. Spoil-Sports

S ports should be done away with, they are rife with negativism, and I don't like negativism.

Nobody enjoys sports—they just pretend to. Did you know that a player leaves the court, arena or field feeling good about his performance only 11.1% of the time?* The other 88.9% of the time he leaves swearing and grumbling.

Let me spell that out—eighty-eight point nine percent!

And you know it's true, don't you? Because you're one of the 88.9%, aren't you? I know I used to be, about 99.9% of the time. 99.9%! Do I need to spell it out for you?

And who is it you're grumbling and swearing at? Yourself. You actually spend your hardly-earned money to endure a couple of hours of frustration, and what for? To work yourself into a fine snit, that's what for.

Going bowling? As a rule, half the time you will bowl under your average. That doesn't make you happy, does it? The other half of the time, you'll bowl over your average. A good percentage of those times you'll still be disappointed because you could have hit a hundred above your average, if only you hadn't dropped your shoulder, broken your stride, failed to follow through, et cetera ad nauseum.

Let's follow through on that follow-through thing for a sec. Follow-through is the most troublesome of bugaboos for a sportster in any sport. Be it golf, bowling, boxing, batting, pitching, horseshoes, tennis, or marriage, follow-through is the key.

I think that skydiving may be the only sport where a good, steady follow-through would be a disadvantage.

On the other hand—well, actually, on both other hands—just "throwing and catching" can be tricky in organized sports. In most games you can throw with either hand, but coaches instruct you to catch with both of them. On the third other hand, it's an offense to use your hands on the offense in football, in soccer—or on a first date.

And what about your head?

What you do with your head varies widely across sports. In golf, you must keep it down. In most other sports, you must keep it up. In boxing, you must keep it from getting knocked off. In swimming, you keep it up, down, up, down, up, down. In racquetball you keep it the hell out of the way. And in baseball and softball, it doesn't matter what you do with your head, as long as you keep the eyeball part of it on the game ball. But in all sports, you are continually advised to use it, and perpetually admonished not to lose it.

Having rushed headlong into that heady diversion, I will now take my own advice and follow through on what I've been trying to say here—and probably succeeding far more superbly than even I realize as is usually the case—which is that the whole sports thing is one big orgy of masochism.

Looking at it that way, marathon running has to be the crumb-de-la-crumb for the numb-de-la-dumb. Not only do you punish yourself for twenty-seven pointless miles, but you have to punish yourself with warm-ups and cool-downs, too. This supposedly assures you of avoiding injuries, so you can keep masochising your body over and over, again and again.

One last word about the word *sport*. Where do you think it comes from? Sounds sorta like Sparta to me. The Spartans lived three millennia ago. They believed in rigorous exercise, austere living and strict discipline. It's said that one of their generals ordered a thousand of his men to march over a cliff to their deaths, just to show a visitor how well-trained and disciplined they were.

So, go ahead, Mr. and Ms. Sporty-Sport-Sport, Just Do It. As for me, I think I'll settle back with a cold one and watch the professional masochists on ESPN. Which will make me part of the 11.1%...

...a thousand percent of the time.

14. Stalking the Wily Pan Fish

I could give you the real names of the seven guys I just spent the weekend fishing with, but for now let's just call them Sleepy, Grumpy, Sleazy, Sneaky, Sloppy, Stoned, and Dork. Like the seven simpering squirts that were their predecessors, their names are not just lyrical, they are descriptive of their personalities.

Even though they do little to accomplish it, those seven stalwarts have one thing in common: their desire to bring home the bacon in the form of a large small-mouth bass, or an even larger large-mouth bass, or a trout worthy of putting on a wall, or a walleye that gave a better fight than a Norwegian sardine, canned or not so.

Not me!

I stalk the wily pan fish. I go for the perch and the sunfish, the crappie and the bluegill—the ones that are easy to catch. So, whereas my friends almost always go home fish fry failures, I very often go home a seafood supper success.

Most of us arrived at *Camp Flying Fish Hooks* at about seven on Friday evening and started unloading supplies. It was at this time that Dork formulated the first of what were to become the now famous Dork's Contorted Corollaries: "Never have the guy who brings the gas can also bring the bread." Especially if his name is Stoned and he puts them in the trunk, together. Friday night's ham sandwiches were on a choice of high-octane white or unleaded rye.

We were still putting stuff away when Sleepy and Grumpy started their weekend-long argument over which color jig—yellow or black—is best for walleye. A moot point since the two of them barely look at the water, except for what's in their chaser glasses. For Grumpy, it's always too hot or too cold or too windy or too late or too early or too whatever to fish, and Sleepy never gets out of bed until Happy Hour. But their argument got the guys started and pretty soon the bets were flying. "A dollar on the first fish, five dollars on the first game fish, five dollars on the largest fish, ten dollars on the most fish..." You can see the chum in the water for a year's dissension and hard feelings, to end just in time for the next annual fishing trip. Would it be the first "keeper" game fish? Longest? Girthiest? Weightiest? If someone started fishing before the rest of us, would it count?

"Hey! Talk about starting early," Grumpy grumbled. "Sleazy and Sneaky have taken off with one of our two camp boats and all the live bait."

The joke really was on Sneaky and Sleazy. Grumpy knew that, but they made his day by giving him another way to live up to his name. Those two slime-balls thought they were getting the drop on the rest of us, but this had to be their first time at a fishing camp. They had yet to learn that the first fundamental of any fishing camp is that you bring bait and tackle to catch fish, you talk about fish, you argue about fish, you make bets about fish. But no one actually wastes the whole weekend fishing.

Hell, there just isn't time for it. Maybe on Saturday afternoon, a few of the guys who are die-hard fishermen and aren't too hung-over, will go out in the boat for a couple of hours. But you can't hit all the lakeside bars—where you talk about fishing, of course—and hold marathon poker games at camp—still talking about fishing—and actually *fish*, too.

Saturday night, or maybe it was Saturday afternoon, though I suppose it could even have been Friday night (it was a very hazy weekend), a bunch of us were in the "CR," which stands for Crossroads Tavern. You have to talk like that when on a fishing trip; it shows you're practically almost a local, now that you've come to this area for two days in a row for two years in a row. We were talking about fishing, naturally, when the proprietor brought out a recently caught, humongous fish from his freezer. We all admired it and then Sloppy, who is fantastic with a devil's-image-catcher-that-will-steal-your-soul-and-damn-you-to-hell-forever-if-you-happen-to-be-Amish box got the bright idea of posing each of us with this petrified Pisces so we could prove to our wives we really did go on a fishing trip and not just on some drunken, carousing, gambling, card-playing, hell-raising weekend.

Sloppy gave us each a print a few days after we got back, and all I can say is, that man is so unbelievable with a shutter, you couldn't tell the fish was frozen—you'd swear it was still wriggling. Good thing too, because it was well after beer-thirty—by that time we fishermen were as limpid as jellyfish in a lava lamp.

To confirm how realistic it was, oh ye of little faith; not too long after that, Sleazy got a nasty letter condemning his lack of sportsmanship from the proprietor of the CR. It seems he didn't think it was as funny as we did when the sports section of the *Herald Journal* newspaper published a picture of Sleazy with his humongous fish.

So we didn't return from our trip with any fish, pan or otherwise, but that didn't matter. We had what we'd really gone after— one helluva fish story.

15. The Great Cowfish

D uring rainy spells I tend to limp a bit, but I wasn't born with a limpabit. It's a legacy from my encounter with the legendary Great Cowfish.

Down on Crystal Lake a number of years ago (before I was born; that shows you how many years back), they had the biggest, meanest catfish anyone had ever seen. Now, everybody knows that catfish can go 30, 40, even 60 pounds, but this one was bigger than that. Much bigger.

Everybody called him *Oscar* but, as my story will show, that was a misnomer. Can't blame people—it's pretty hard for most humans to tell the hims from the hers in the fish world, and the rest are just guessing.

The reason I know about all this is that my granddaddy, Jake, kept a farm along the lake and he had a Brahma bull. Like the catfish, Oscar, he was the biggest and meanest of his ilk in all Hillsdale County—and not just the orneriest, but also the horneriest.

Naturally, Grandpa Jake named him *Old Horny*.

Now, if you know fish, you know that when winter sets in, bullhead and other catfish burrow down into the mud and hibernate until spring. This one spring, the lake was uncommonly low because winter had been very mild and the spring rains were late.

By the time the first warm rain did come—and a good catfisherman knows it's that first warm rain that wakes 'em up—Oscar was stuck in the dirt pretty far above water level. She struggled to free herself as the rain turned the hard dirt to mud, and finally got her tail loose. She was wiggling it for all she was worth when Old Horny spotted her. Not being one to pass up a lady in distress, he had his way with her.

Apparently, bulls don't have the same problem we have figuring out the sex of a fish.

Later that year, Oscar birthed the first and only Great Cowfish known to man. Lest ye doubt me, let me point out that stranger things have been birthed, like the Pegasus, the Cyclops, and Pee Wee Herman, just to name a few.

The Cowfish grew and grew. Every time anyone spotted it, it had gotten exponentially bigger. Folks started calling it *Orson Swells* (there's that gender identification problem again) although some people did try calling her *Mama Bass*, it didn't catch. Either way, a rose is a rose is a rose, so let's just say that it grew to humongous size, with horns wider than the fins on the Batmobile.

Years later, when my granddaddy died, he willed me his boots—the most beautiful handmade boots you've ever seen. Only one thing wrong with them; they were size 14, and there I was in my early teens and only a size 9.

Didn't matter, I wore 'em everywhere.

And I was wearing them the day I decided that I was going to catch Orson-Kate. I had sharpened up a small anchor to use as a hook, bought 20 feet of heavy duty tow chain for fishing line, and had a few boa constrictors, pythons, and so on in my bait pail. Nothing was working, though, until I put on the rattler. Musta been the vibration of the rattle that got Kate-Orson's goat, 'cause that chain was zingin' out between my feet so fast it was striking up sparks.

When the chain was just about all played out, I pulled way back to set the hook.

That was a big mistake.

Before I knew what was happening, my boots took off with my feet still in 'em and I was skimming across the lake on my heels like I was water-skiing, up the lake, down the lake, and up the lake again.

After about two hours, Or-Kate-Son Swells-Smith led me into the South Jackson Road swamp area and made one great turn of the bay. I felt like I was end-man on a roller-skating whip. The chain snapped and I slammed into a bunch of weeds, hit the shore, and was flung arse-over-teakettle right up onto the highway. I landed arse-on-the-asphalt just in time to be run over by a plumber who stopped long enough to say he was in a hurry because he'd told a woman he'd fix her leaky faucet that afternoon and he didn't want to be late, then he took off, the bastard.

My leg was busted in three places. It took some hospital time, and some rehab exercises, but young boys heal fast. Now, you'd never know I got hurt, except when it rains and I start to limp.

I know, I know, you think I'm having you on, pulling your leg, yanking your chain, but I swear to you, it is as true as it is unbelievable—that plumber was going to fix that lady's sink on the very day he said he would!

Amazing, isn't it?

I entered this fable in a liars contest in Summerset, Michigan and placed second. The person who took first place had told a true story. Funny, but true. I argued with the judges that his story didn't meet the qualification of being a lie, by virtue of it being true. They were having none of it, though, damn hicks!

16. White-Water Derby

I t was spring, and Starr was jumping up and down like a little kid. "Let's go to the white-water canoe races in North Creek, Artie! Let's go to the white-water canoe races in North Creek! Can we, Artie? Huh? Can we? Huh? Huh? Can we?" It was an event she'd attended a few times before we met, and she'd enjoyed herself immensely.

I figured, why not?

I'll tell you why not.

Because my elevator doesn't go all the way to the top, that's why not. Because I never think things through, that's why not. Because I hate cold so much, I actually use those tiny ice tongs that no one else bothers with. That's why not. And yet, here I was, in effect saying, "Sure! Let's head north to the frozen tundra of the Upper Hudson, where we can stand on a precipice in the icy wind for a few hours. It'll be fun!"

After driving for over three hours, I saw a sight that no man should ever see — at least, not on the first weekend of May.

At first, I was mystified.

Then, I was horrified.

It was...*snow!*

Snow!

In May!

Undaunted, — well, I was daunted, but if you think Starr was daunted, well, you daunt know her at all — we forged on to the lodge that my brother-in-law Roger had rented with three of his friends. Now, I wasn't expecting four-star amenities. Starr did tell me that the facilities were *pee by the tree* and *bath by the path*. But there were other details that she held close to her ample vest that, although I do love her ample vest, I wish she'd have mentioned. Things like the lodge being three miles up a rut-filled goat path, or the water was by *bail and pail*, and the heating was by *wedge and sledge*.

But, hey, I'm a fungi, and we were a fungroup; so a shot of backwoods living was gamely toasted by laugh and gaff, shrug and hug, with a mug and jug chaser, by one and all.

I stopped laughing and gaffing when I found out that Roger and his friends intended to enter two canoes in the race. I know that probably doesn't shock you, but I haven't told you the really asinine part yet—they were going to be *in* those canoes. I began to suspect that this crew's elevator didn't go to the top *or* the bottom of the shaft, it didn't even go up and down—if it went anywhere at all, it went sideways.

The water in the Upper Hudson is barely warmer than the glaciers that birthed it, and those glaciers left rocks. No, not rocks; boulders. We're talkin' canoe-chewers and kayak-shellackers here, folks. Not to mention the hull-holers, side-splitters, rudder-cutters and manhood-maimers, all waiting a mere six inches below the surface.

Suddenly, shivering on the sidelines sounded a lot more appealing.

I bought an official program that was about as informative as an FBI agent. I learned that the course was laid out in such a way that spectators don't get to see the beginning of the race. That happens way upriver. All we could 'spect to spectatorate was the end of the race.

What I didn't learn was what the rules were. Were the craft launched by class, or in mixed groups with each craft being individually timed, or in heats? Who knew? Were they penalized for spills, above and beyond the pain inflicted by nature? If they fell out of the craft, could they get back into the craft—if they were damn fool enough to want to get back into the craft—and if they *could* get back into the craft—were they allowed to continue to the finish?

The program answered none of these questions, and many more—which ended up being endemic to the entire endeavor.

Case in point—before coming up to North Creek, Roger had

called the local Chamber of Commerce to see what they had to do to qualify. He was told all they had to do was show up on the day of the race and register. But when they did that, they were informed that they were too late; their entries should have been mailed one week in advance.

The rules of entry in the program, such as they were, listed no such proviso.

I got the feeling that the people who were managing this race were the same ones who oversaw the building of Chernobyl. But I guess, to be fair, they shouldn't be expected to have worked out all of the kinks in the mere twenty-five years they've been holding the event.

Watching the race near the finish line, I saw a mixture of canoes, kayaks, rafts, floats and dinghies. Some had but a single pilot, others had several. There was even one guy in an inner tube! You read me right—a man in an inner tube, with his arms, legs and kiester in water that was so cold (*how cold was it?*) that if a basso profundo were to dangle his organ of benevolence in it for half a beat, he would become a soprano for life.

The race itself was a mishmash of unbridled chaos and anarchy. I guess I was the only viewer of the thousands who was bothered by all this. It seemed to me that most of the spectators didn't give a damn tinker who won. They just came to watch some whip flip his ship and immediately try to convince God that his re-entry into the fold and staying on the straits and narrows were synonymous concepts.

Starr and I watched in the cold and rain for three fill-in-the-blank-with-your-favorite-curse-word hours.

Thoroughly chilled, I finally convinced her that we couldn't stand any more fun, and suggested we take a short break. So we hopped into the car, and with me behind the wheel, drove off to find a hot toddy.

After the first hour on the road, she realized that the hot toddy I was aiming for was in a warm friendly tavern...all the way back home in Syracuse.

17. The Argo, Not

I bought the *Argo* when my eldest daughter announced her intention to move from Syracuse to New Jersey. I remember thinking, "Well, this is the first one, and I suppose all seven will eventually move on. Who knows when we'll all get together again for a family vacation?" So I bought the boat to entice them to spend two weeks at a rented camp on Black Lake, water-skiing, fishing, boating and swimming.

The name of the boat had nothing to do with Jason and his Argo-nuts. I named it after an old knock-knock punchline "...*Argo* take a flying leap at a rolling doughnut!"

I bought the boat for vacation use, but prudence dictated that I take it out on a trial run. (I always hated Prudence, that control freak. But when she's right, she's right.) I told Starr what I was doing in the note I left behind, but she would have known anyway. Starr's not stupid.

My favorite nephew, Rocky, and I launched the *Argo* from Bridgeport and spent the afternoon fishing. Three sunfish, two perch and one rock bass later, we had hit the legal limit, so we started for shore. Clever boy that I am, I asked Rocky to pull the drain plug "and the water will drain out while we head in!"

I bet you wish you had my smarts, don't you?

When we were a few yards from shore, I told him to put the plug back in.

"I don't have it," he said. "It must be with you."

"'Taint." (That's how edumacated people talk.)

"'Tis." (Rocky's not educated, but he likes to pretend he is.)

After a couple of rousing rounds of this, I said, "Well, we've gotta plug it with something. You got anything?"

"Nope."

"This will have to do then," I decided. And I stripped off my swimming trunks.

And wouldn't you know it: just at that moment a car pulled into the boat launch and out stepped a state trooper and, I assumed, his daughter, who was about twelve years old. I immediately scanned the boat looking for something, anything to cover up with. But if we'd had anything else, it would be stuffed in the boat's bunghole, and *my* bunghole would already be covered.

My choices were my fishing pole or my tackle box.

So there I was, sitting in a boat that was slowly floating in circles, steering with one hand while trying my best not to let the open tackle box slip off my lap. I couldn't switch seats with my nephew without asking the young lady which view she preferred—ding-dong or derrière.

Then I noticed that the trooper had walked over to the nearest tree and was taking a whiz!

I toyed with the idea of making a citizen's arrest for indecent exposure. Fortunately for him, they left when he was done doing his business, leaving me to do mine—docking in the leaking boat, that is; not leaking in the docking boat.

A few days later, having bought a new plug for the boat, I set off with the family on the much-anticipated trip.

I allowed each of my kids to invite a friend, and my buddy Rum decided to join us, too, with his wife and one-year-old son (my godson), as well as his wife's kid sister. If you thought fifteen children and four adults made the dinner table look like da Vinci's "Last Supper," you should have peeked in at bedtime. Bodies were stacked like cordwood.

In order to feed this horde, anyone who could hold a pole was sent down to the lake to fish, with instructions that, "If a man with a beard and seven platitudes stops by and offers to bless the fish, don't discourage him."

A few days into our family vacay, I took all who wanted to go, horseback riding. Considering we were bringing her ten or twelve riders, I was able to work out a good deal with the stable-owner beforehand. She was glad to get our business.

She stationed her nine-year-old son in the corral to help the kids mount. She stationed Rum and I at the big barn doors, with instructions to let only one horse through the doors at a time, and to wait until the next rider was mounted before the previous rider rode out. She would be saddling the horses and settling the riders.

Before we knew it, a half a dozen horses were stampeding towards the barn door and us, and I tell you, those beasts were much larger than I'd thought. They had to be at least ninety hands high! (Horses are measured in hands, not hooves, er, feet. Don't ask me why.)

Rum hollered, "Save yourself, Art. I'm outta here!" And he swung his body around so the door was between him and the blood-thirsty brutes.

No braver than he, I did the same. And of course, of course, the nine-year-old horse-boy came to the rescue of the two grown coward-men, grabbing the reins of all six killer equines at once, and sweet-talking them out of their homicidal rage. *Equus!*

Despite our lack of horse-sense, everyone had such a good time we all went riding again the next day.

Yup, the first week was going wonderfully well. The lake was beautiful. The fishing was beautiful. The weather was extraordinarily beautiful. There was, however, one clump of seaweed in our seaway of joy: my infant godson. That kid started crying the very first day, and he never stopped. Oh man, did he cry! He cried all day, all night and every second in between. I'm sorry to say it, but that infant was ruining the vacation for everyone. And he wasn't having much fun, either.

So Rum's wife called her mother. "Mom, remember how you said you never get enough time with the baby? Well how about a whole ten days of infantile bliss?"

Rum and I made the trip to Syracuse with Sir Squalls-A-Lot, toot suite. The only stops allowed were piss breaks by the side of the road. When we reached our destination we stayed just long enough to unload the little bundle of joy, and skedaddled before his grandmother got wise.

On the way back we had a more leisurely ride, stopping at

every tavern for Rum to tinkle, because he was blessed by God with an itsy-bitsy bladder. Our progress became progressively slower, because of course we had to have a drink or six at each pee-stop in order to thank the owners for having the foresight to place their tavern so strategically.

We picked up a twenty-year-old hitch-hiking girl in Adams Center. She was wearing a see-through blouse, see-through shorts and even see-through shoes (sandals).

If you have trouble digesting that last paragraph, see *A True Fisherman*...on previous pages.

We two too-stewed tomatoes arrived back at camp at about the same time God was deciding whether or not it was worth his while to cause yet another unwitnessed by me sunrise. I'll assume it was.

The rest of the vacation went swimmingly; water-skiing, fishing, campfires, wasps, poison ivy, rainy day board games—the perfect mix for what, thankfully, was *not* our last family get-to-gether as I had feared—though it certainly was one of the most memorable.

The Artful Codger

1. A Call to Arms

The Great White Hunter no longer stalks the wily beasts of the beastly wilds, it's true, but that doesn't mean he's cased his guns. No, that isn't the case by any means.

The Great White Hunter is neither dead nor disappeared. He has been urbanized.

I know this for a fact because he lives right next door to me and his name is Ashton Badgley. As long as he's been in the neighborhood, Ashton has waged a one-man battle to eradicate the area of dangerous predators, a list including but not exclusive to panthers, boa constrictors and alligators.

You see, a few years ago our local paper did such a good job reporting sightings of a black panther, she became a Central New York legend. And there were always rumors of an alligator or a snake (pick one) that had broken out of the zoo or was flushed down the toilet (pick one) and had grown into a huge, hungry snake-a-gator that traveled throughout the city sewer system terrorizing toddlers, terriers and the occasional neighborhood watch guy (pick two).

My point is (in case you didn't think I was ever going to get to one) you haven't heard those rumors in quite a while, have you? And it was exactly quite a while ago that Ashton Badgley moved into our neighborhood.

Coincidence? Not according to Ashton Badgley.

According to Ashton Badgley, Ashton Badgley has single-handedly obliterated all the panthers, boa constrictors and herpigators in town. And given the fact that Ashton Badgley's only weapon is a BB gun, it's amazing how successful Ashton Badgley's been...so far.

But now he faces the most vicious varmint of them all, the Columbia Livia: A.K.A. The all-invasive, all-pervasive American Pigeon.

But can one man defeat this monumental defiler of monuments and so much more? Town after town has tried to stop the onslaught of the city pigeon to no avail. Yet, our new Red Rider and his trusty BB gun fight on.

He knows his enemies. He knows their tactics. He even knows their names.

There's Big Burd (the second B is pronounced like a T); Messerschmidt (the second M is optional); Rock Dove (not hard to figure that one out), and; The Red Baron (definitely more fecund than barren). And the leader of the whole fracking flock is Little White Dove, who assumed command when Walter, the most famous Pigeon ever, was optioned to a seven-picture deal with MGM. (Which was quite a feather in their cap.)

Don't let Little White Dove's name fool you. She's the best feces-flinging flapper of the lot; tracking her target (usually me) and striking with the pinpoint accuracy of an unmanned drone.

This all reminds me of the story about the two psychiatric patients sitting on the crazy-house lawn. An old hand was telling a newcomer to watch out for the real crazies.

"You can tell who they are," he said, "because they always dress in white and have keys."

Just then, Little White Dove's big sister flew over and plopped a big one right on the new guy's head. An attendant rushed over, saying, "Don't move, I'll get some toilet paper."

"See what I mean?" said the veteran. "By the time she gets back that bird will be *miles* away!"

Knowing the foe that Badgley faces and the odds against him, I'm ashamed to admit I've left this brave man to fight alone. So deep is my shame, I have actually been moved to action. Action! Me! You see how serious this is?

I've been practicing nightly with my boy's slingshot. For weeks I have honed my skill, and in the process rid my own yard of vicious vermin. Now, with nary a slug nor a snail left in my lawn, I am ready to take my place slightly behind the Great White Hunter.

And you? Are you ready to defend you home, your town, your very *coif* from this avian nightmare? Well, okay, then! Load your pockets with stones and BBs, my friend. Load up your water pistol; put new rubbers on your slingshots. Do whatever you must, but whatever you do, don't wait until it's too late and we're all up to our armpits in pigeon-shit.

For, as Wilhelm Shite-speare might once have written:

> To help or not to help, what was the question?
> Whether 'tis neighborly to suffer the flings of sparrows'
> Outrageous droppings, or to take arms
> Against a sea of bird-turds, and, by slinging shot, end
> them.

2. A Funny Thing Happened on the Way to the Crematorium

If you're famous when you die, the newspapers will print your picture for free. If not, someone else will have to pay. If you're really famous—like FDR or JFK—they'll devote whole pages of pictures to you and your family. Well, actually, in FDR's case, half of the papers did photo spreads on his wife Eleanor, and the other half did spreads on his dog, Fala. But that's really a moot point—nobody could tell the difference.

As a rule, Presidents who make a great impact before ascending to the Great Caucus in the Sky are accorded special treatment. Those who don't—like Pierce and Ford—aren't. As a matter of fact, I remember Walter Cronkite making this announcement when Ford passed away: "We have information from a fairly reliable source that someone died last night." Reagan thought he meant Henry Ford, after all, even Gerald's own kin didn't realize he hadn't been attending family functions. They just assumed he was still stumbling around on the golf links trying to make par.

I've noticed a trend in these presidential post-part-em pictures: they all seem to me to have been taken decades before the deceased shuffled off their mortal coil. As if that desiccated carcass was not truly the man, but rather the in-the-prime-of-his-life fellow pictured in the paper.

I've never suffered from the venality of vanity. I brush my teeth, I comb my hair, I don't mix stripes with prints: that's about it. But I *have* designated the photo I want printed with my obituary. It's not a picture of me as a father, surrounded by my adoring children; nor of me as a husband, surrounded by my adoring wives; nor even of me as an entrepreneur, surrounded by somewhat less adoring customers.

It's me as a gap-toothed five-year-old, riding on my tricycle.

Was there ever a happier, more care-free time than when I was vroom-vroom-vrooming around the sidewalks of my home block? Old playing cards pinned to the spokes of the over-sized front wheel would make a slappa-slappa noise that sounded like the tires of passing automobiles. I had pedals, and handlebars to steer with, and a horn! I had a *vehicle!* (No, I didn't know the word "vehicle" yet, but I knew what I *had*.) I could make it go or stop or turn at my will, and a city-block's worth of sidewalk to race up and down.

My own private *Autobahn*.

The world has tarnished and diminished the free spirit that was once within each of us, but maybe that is the self that should be remembered.

As for how he wanted to be remembered, my father-in-law, Bob, always said that he wanted a speaker hooked up to the kneeling bench in the funeral parlor, so that he could greet each mourner with "Thank you so much for coming!" (Damn it, Bob, I should have done that for you. It was the least I could do; after all you gave me your daughter, Starr, the love of my life. Sorry old boy—maybe next time.)

For myself, I've always said *in comicus sancti*, so I hereby request that my heirs, consigns and concubines refuse entry to my wake to anyone without a joke to tell. That way, at least the tears (and groans) that follow the punch lines of my comically-impaired friends will mask the one or two real tears (or groans) that my mourners might shed. And while they sob and squabble over the top-shelf whiskey, let them do so under the eyes of that happy five-year-old me.

On my trike. Owning the world.

3. Alexander Graham Belge

*C*esar Milan, where were you when I needed you?

Starr has always been fond of big, dumb animals, so one Christmas I bought her a Saint Bernard and we became a two leash family. (If you can't figure it out, I'll pray for you.)

For naming rights on our new bumble of joy, our daughter Sammy committed to being his main cleaner-upper for one week. She chose "Alexander Graham Belge," which, of course, was soon shortened to "Dammit."

If you've ever had a Saint Bernard, then you already know they're among the gentlest and strongest of breeds. They're also clumsy—very, very clumsy. And they are stupid—very, very stupid. So stupid that they don't even know they are so very, very clumsy. And they are large—very, very large. Thus a Saint Bernard goes through life thinking he's as graceful as a swan when he's actually more like a bull with a bee under its tail—sort of a Gene Kelly *esprit* trapped in a Hulk Hogan *de corps*.

To give you an example, when we called Alex from the living room for supper, he would have to go through the dining room and make a right turn into the kitchen. The first time he was called, he didn't realize that the dining room floor was polished hardwood, and when he tried to make the turn his feet pumped a mile a minute towards the kitchen, but his body continued in a straight line until he smashed snout-first into the dining room wall. Now, anyone can make a mistake. But Alex performed this ritual every night thereafter without fail. Saint Alexander the Bonehead had fewer smarts than his doggy dish and a worse memory than Ronnie Reagan, rest his soul.

I guess you can't blame him: after all, Saint Bernards were bred to be strong, not bright, just strong. Our mistake was trying to keep such a big dog in the city. They need lots of room. The country is best—one the size of China, preferably.

I built a fence. He jumped the fence.

I built the fence higher.

Starr watched out the kitchen window as he perched on top of the fence like Snoopy imitating a vulture, and rocked back and forth until he tumbled to the ground on the other side. Clearly amazed at his success, he lifted his head and let out a triumphant bark of freedom, then trotted off, hot on the scent of our school-bound children.

I built the fence even higher and even stronger. He rammed it and rammed it until he annihilated the whole bloody thing—including the two eight-inch gate posts.

He didn't want to be in the yard. He wanted to be in school with the kids, happily running up and down the halls, clumsily smashing into walls, people and (uh, oh!) the principal. This gave the principal two problems: One, keeping our kids in school and two, keeping Alex out. He didn't have any more success with the first than the Border Patrol has in San Diego; but he was determined to accomplish the second.

To this end, he would call the dogcatcher when Alex followed the kids to school, and then they'd play Catch Me If You Can running up and down the school halls. The principal could not catch Alex when he was playfully galumphing through the halls.

Nor could his vice principal.

Nor could the rest of the faculty, the whole student body, the janitor, the secretary, all the king's horses or the cast of Benny Hill, all combined. But the dogcatcher? No sweat! That stupid galoot would hop right into his wagon. It turned out school-galumphing took a back seat to car-riding on Alex's list any day. (Sorry, I'm just too geared up to put the brakes on a hard-driving pun.)

To improve his behavior, Starr took Alex to obedience school—where the top dog (that is, the trainer) accepted Alex, but disqualified Starr. You see, they have this special collar called a choke chain. If the dog doesn't do exactly as you wish, you simply give the leash a good yank with one hand and the choke chain rips his head off. Now that you have his attention, he's much more likely to notice the pistol in your other hand, thus spurring him on to heights of obedience that you could never reach with your children. Not even if they were studying under the loving lash of the Grand Inquisitor, Torquemada, himself.

That's how it was supposed to work. But when Starr yanked on his choke chain, Alex would just stare up at her with his big eyes, his tongue drooling and lolling to one side, panting as if to say "Did you want something?"

The head hound-cho at doggy school suggested that Starr get someone stronger to train the beast, so I went along with the gag and picked up the doggy duty for my beloved, even though I've seen her arm-wrestle truck drivers for draft beers—and win.

After about three re-enlistments in the school, Alex was doing pretty well. He had me heeling and coming when he barked—no, actually, he was doing quite well. He would come when he was called. He would keep his place half a step behind me just like Starr had trained me to do with her. But he still hadn't overcome one other serious fault—and that was attacking bitches. Let him see or smell one and he was off, snarling and barking, and saying words in doggy-talk that I was pretty sure did not mean, "Fine day, isn't it, Ma'am, shall we take a stroll?"

One Sunday morning, Starr and I were out walking Alex when an alluring collie of the female persuasion appeared down the block. Alex's ears pricked up and his body got tense. I could sense that her pheromones were causing his hormones to spike his libido. (Or would that be that libidog?)

Usually when this happened, Alex would go charging after his quarry, dragging me behind, hanging on for dear life. But I was determined that this was going to stop. Today he would get his final lesson. I would slacken his choke-chain, and when he was ready to take off he would have lots of room to start his run. Then—whammo!—I would yank back so hard that I'd send him back to his litter days.

So, there the collie was, preening; there Alex was, panting; and there I was, gripping the loose chain with both fists.

The collie barked.

Alex bolted.

I yanked with all my might.

And lo and behold, Alex stopped cold.

Unfortunately, I did not. That split-second wasn't enough for my brain to process the fact that the chain had gone slack. So my fists continued their downward arc until they slammed right into my groin.

Suddenly, his coup de grace became my coup de grapes, if you'll pardon my Françoise.

Hands clutching my banana split, I writhed on the sidewalk, shouting every verboten word in the Anglo-Saxon lexicon. Right on cue, two elderly ladies coming back from church stepped out of their car just in time to look down on this maniac, cussing out a poor, sweet Saint Bernard.

In the end, we had to admit that our Big Galoot was too big for our small city. This cat needed galumphing room. So Starr paid for boarding at The Humane Society, and asked them to find a home for him, hopefully in the country.

Several months later Starr told me she got a call from Alex's new owners. They loved him dearly, and said that he loved living in the country, and they wanted to breed him.

Many years later my son told me that when he'd gone to school and told his friends we'd given our dog to people who lived on a farm, his friends told him that was what all parents told their kids when they've had their dog put down. "It stood to reason," he said, "that no farm could be *that* big!"

I asked Starr about this, but all she did was smile a Mona Lisa smile and drink a fifth, er, plead The Fifth.

Come to think of it, I'll bet that's why the kids always flew off like bats out of hell whenever I asked them if they wanted to go for a ride in the country.

4. Cabaret

In summertimes long ago, in the early evening when it was still light out, the voices of the neighborhood kids would carry through the open window of my childhood home. The pull to join my friends was so compelling I can still feel its intensity through the decades. The laughter and joyful shouts told me where the fun was, and if that was where the fun was, that was where I wanted to be. Any delay meant not only missing a little of the fun, but the certainty of losing the best time of my life, forever.

Is that why I go to the taverns now? Is it because that's where the 'kids' are? Where the fun is? Or at least where the possibility of fun to be missed is? Granted, there are good times in the bar with camaraderie, games and laughs. But many times—most times—bars are about as exciting as bus terminals.

Yet, I go. And I sit there, bored.

And I chat with boring people—people who are probably talking to me because their more entrancing friends are elsewhere. *Anywhere* elsewhere.

Bored, I leave, not wanting to admit that there might be something lacking in me. And so I visit the next tavern on the pike. For what? Other kids to play with? Maybe I should flip a coin. Heads, I go to a harpsichord recital. Tails, I commit suicide. (I refuse to do both; my body doesn't need that much punishment. And in my considerably biased opinion, they're pretty much the same thing.)

Alone we are born. Alone we die. In between, we live. Look around. The world is filled with lonely people, and we are they. Welcome to the cabaret.

5. Damn Nuns

*T*wo things that have always given me greif are speling and... one other thing. Since I'm talking about just myself, and not all men, I have obviously excluded two other things that give me grief: bosses and wives. Which one might reasonably argue are the same thing. If, however, you are in the habit of arguing unreasonably, people will have a valid reason not to want to argue with you. But on the other hand, if you only operate from invalid reasoning, you should be in a sanitarium. (Shouldn't that be "insanitarium"?)

Let's get back to my problems. What were they, again? Oh yes; bad mammary and pour spelling. On this subject, one example always comes to mind. Every time I use the word "necessary" I have to check the dictionary to c how many cees (see? one c!) and esses (two!) are in it. Now, damnitall, if I can remember that example, why can't I just remember how to spell the word?

I have a brother-in-law who can go through a group of fifty people and give each one's name without uttering a single er, um, or mumble. And, so-help-me-Janus, I have looked over his shoulder and there is no list. No, not so much as a cheat-sheet or a ballpoint note on his palm. He does it all by memory.

And people wonder why "in-law" has become a dirty word.

You might say it's all mnemonics, but we both know that's horse hockey, don't we? (By the way, the "m" in mnemonics, like the "x" in xsycho, is silent. I think.) Let's say we meet someone named Rosenbloom who has a big nose; so we make a mental note to remember that big nose equals nose-in-bloom equals Rosenbloom. A week later when we meet him again, what do our short-circuiting synapses dredge out?

"How nice to see you again, Mr. Durante!"

Which brings me to the heart of my problem: I don't seem to be able to remember the names of things. I have seven children, and unless I name them chronologically, I will point, snap my fingers repeatedly, and utter unintelligible grunts. Thus, all of my children—even my singular son—are known as "Kassykaylanesambutchwindymarsha."

On occasion, I have not only forgotten I was married (for which Starr delivers her own mnee-monic device, a kick in the... shin)—but I've even forgotten my wife's first name. And believe me, I'd rather have a kick in the...shin...than the look I got on that occasion. *That* look could have roasted...marshmallows.

I swear, if some hardware manufacturer would start naming their items whatsits, thingamabobs and whozits instead of turn-buckles, molly-bolts and unions, (or did I want connectors?) they'd make a fortune.

By this time you're probably thinking, "sounds like Alzhei-mer's to me, and Art's not using that word because he can't remember it—much less speel it." Well, if that's the case, then it must be early Alzheimer's—very early, because I've had it all my life. The only reason I didn't start speaking until I was three years old was that I kept forgetting the words 'mama' and 'dada'.

And even if you're not thinking that or not wondering if I spelled Alzheimer's correctly, I know you *are* wondering what any of this has to do with nuns. Let's see; it had something to do with something, and...what was I saying?

6. Fear of Flying

A ny psychiatrist worth her Psyche will tell you that it's perfectly normal to have a phobia or two. And any statistician worth his static will tell you that out of all the professions, psychiatry has the second highest rate of suicide.

And what do these things tell us?

For one thing, they tell us that most psychiatrists don't suffer from *necrophobia*; the morbid fear of mortality. For another thing, it tells us that few of the very same ego-ologists who obsess over unraveling our tangled ids have their own heads on straight.

Meanwhile, these self-same, suicidal psychiatrists will tell you that it's normal and even advisable to have at least one good phobia to fall back on—just as long as you don't get carried away and pick something really, really weird like *phobophobia*, the fear of fear. And you certainly don't want *aichmophobia*, the fear of sharp objects, because a serious phobia such as that takes at least a year and a half to learn how to spell.

Like anyone else, I have my fears, my phobias, and stuff I'm a-scared of.

The worst of my fears is *acrophobia*, the fear of high places, which I do my best to control. To be honest, my travels seldom take me to places any higher than the mean elevation of the Florida peninsula, so control is not that big an issue. Actually, the thing that gets to me is this: if I'm so afraid of heights, why do I get a strong urge to *Jump! Jump! Jump!* every time I find myself standing on anything taller than a soapbox?

It occurs to me that the call to leap might be emanating from my readers, concentrating their collective ESP with a Big Apple cheer of *Jump! Jump! Jump!* trying to get me to *Nosedive! Nosedive! Nosedive!* off the ledge like a broke and broken Wall Street broker. If this *is* coming from my fans, I would appreciate it if you would knock it off. And I mean *both* of you.

Now then, as I was saying, my acrophobia does not control me, I control it.

Uh oh! That's what addicts say when they're in denial. That must mean that I'm not afraid of heights; I'm addicted to them. I guess that would be called *acrophilia*. I'll have to drop in on a meeting of Acrophiliacs Anonymous. "Hello. My name is Art, and I'm an acrophiliac: I get high on heights." By the way, if there's such a word as "acrophilia," it's Greek to me; I just made it up.

Having suffered long as I have long suffered, I can tell you there is only one thing you can do to protect yourself when you have a serious phobia: learn its proper name and spelling. Because if you can speak intelligently about your fear, you will no longer be perceived as just another nut who's afraid of, say, cats.

"I'm not a 'fraidy-cat,'" you announce to all who'll listen. "I happen to suffer from chronic ailurophobia."

"Hmm," they'll say as they yawn, stretch languidly, and lap up their beer from white saucers.

"That's right," you continue. "And did you know that the word *ailurophobia* comes from the Latin for blah, blah, blah and so forth and so on, et cetera, et cetera, et tu, Brute?"

How's that for an ice-breaker?

But seriously; you drop that tongue-twisting bombshell of Latin lingo legerdemain in casual conversation just once and don't be surprised if your local bartender starts a collection jar to pay for your ongoing therapy.

It turns out people love to give to causes with exotic names. I remember one time I put an old tin can out on the counter at my restaurant. It was labeled Arturo's Indolence Fund. I made a mint.

Besides, if you can call the psychiatrist's office and say, "Hey Doc, I would have made an appointment, but I have *anthrophobia*. That's A-N-T-H-R-O-P-H-O-B-I-A, the fear of people," and hang up before she can respond, you'll save yourself a lot of time and money. You do know what these lobe-lopping head shrinkers get paid, don't you?

Now we're getting to the nub of it.

For the longest time in my youth I thought I had *altophobia* because that was how *acrophobia* was pronounced by my pals in the pool hall. But my Latin teacher, Sister Simon Puella-Puer of the Unholy Order of the Conjugated Word, clucked a nunnish cluck. "Tsk tsk, Arthur. Root words, root words; learn your root words. For instance, people who are *claustrophobic* are deathly afraid of *closets*. And, Arthur, it's high time you learned—there is no such thing as *altophobia*."

"Well, if that were true, sic ergo sum," I cogitated to myself. "I must no longer be afraid of heights! Whoopee!" I immediately tested this theory by clambering up four flights of stairs to the bell tower, where I gazed dizzily down at the kids playing in the schoolyard, far, far below.

I like to think that they enjoyed my lunch as much the second time around as I did the first.

Either way, it was obvious I still had a fear of heights, whatever it was called. So then I thought, well, if I don't have *altophobia*, I must have *aerophobia*. Yup, that's what I've got, I'll betcha! But no, Sister Mary Simon said *aerophobia* is the fear of winds.

My wife tells me she suffers terribly from *aerophobia*, but only on nights when I've been out drinking. And she has good reason. She knows when I get home the force of my flatulence is likely to surpass the destructive power of a category 700 hurricane. It's utter devastation. She also says I'm full of more hot air than an elephant's patootie. But I let that pass.

After long last, Sister Simon got it through my thick skull that what I had was *acrophobia*; and I've had it ever since. I've also got *aviophobia*, the fear of flying, which I'm pretty sure is severely aggravated by my *acrophobia*.

But, wait! As I flip through the Big, Big Book of Fears, Phobias and Other Scary Words, I suddenly realize I'm not really afraid of flying, after all. No, what really turns my lips into slobbering slabs of baby beef liver—and what keeps me from jumping when the urge strikes—is *baso-aglio-thantophobia*; the perfectly rational fear of falling, sustaining massive bodily injuries, and dying a horrible,

horrible death. Which is a long way of saying..*I'm normal.*

Betcha didn't see that coming, did you?

(And in case you're wondering which profession has the highest rate of suicide, and I know you are, it's Police Officers — and I'm afraid of them, too.)

7. Cola War

An extremely attractive lady walked into Arturo's late in the afternoon on a recent Friday and asked for me. Wiping my hands on my apron as I came from the kitchen, I greeted her.

She said, "Hello, sir. I'm from the Trade Research Department of Coca Cola. I would like a few minutes of your time, if I may."

Normally, I wouldn't pass up the chance to pass the time with such a passable person, but I was in the middle of a fish fight, having just started cleaning twenty pounds of monk fish. When I explained, she offered to come back to the kitchen with me and talk while I worked.

What she didn't know was that after a monk fish is skinned, there's still a slimy membrane to remove that's about as easy to strip off as a wet-suit, two sizes too small. So, I was up to my elbows in fish gut yucky-poo-ness, sweating, and smelling about as ripe as an outhouse on a tuna boat. No matter how gorgeous she was (and, boy, she was) I just wasn't in the mood for company. I would explain and she would simply have to understand.

"Okay," I said, "come on back."

She followed while informing me that the Coca Cola Company had a complaint that one of our staff had served a customer Pepsi Cola when they had requested a Coke.

Well, that about did it for me. I wanted names, dates, ranks and serial numbers. I immediately called a carpenter and instructed him to start building a crucifix. Up until that moment I thought watching things like portion control, quality control, inventory control, cash control, bladder control and so on were my big worries—I mean, things that could actually make or break me.

But here we were, talking about serving Pepsi to someone who asked for a Coke—my god, *someone could have been converted!*

I mean, yeah, it's all fun and games till someone *loses a customer.*

I threw myself on the mercy of the cork. I said, "Wait. Before you do anything, I think you should know there could be some mitigating circumstances. It's possible that a new employee, suffering from a rum-and-Coke hangover," (I threw that in for brownie points), "might have goofed. I know it wasn't one of our veteran staff, because every Monday we hold bomb, fire, and "I'm sorry, we don't have Coke, will Pepsi be okay?" drills. A few years back we had a fellow who did okay on the first two, but he never developed his Coke habit. One Saturday night, because of his carelessness, we had to rush several customers up to St. Joe's to have their stomachs pumped. Well, that did it. His fellow staff members held an intervention. If you want to see him, you'll find his skeleton hanging out by the delivery door. I was going to take it down but the Employee Committee said to leave it as a warning to others."

"So, maybe that was it," I said. "A new employee..."

She cut me off, sternly advising me that was no excuse. Coca Cola simply could not allow such infringement on their trademark. It was a "No excuses, *Sir!*" situation. My ass was grass and she was Cheech and Chong's hookah.

This got my hackles up. 'Tis a frightful sight to behold, deep red and purplish-black, angry, engorged hackles swelling to the bursting point, rising from the nape like a banshee from a swamp. Once you've seen it, you'll never forget it. I went on the offensive.

"*Who* complained?"

"That's confidential."

"How many complaints did you receive?"

"I don't know, that's handled in Atlanta."

"Do you have anything in writing?"

"No."

"Then how do you know you're even at the right place?"

After she left, several of the pundits who hang out at Arturo's because no other local dives will have them, started in:

"One hard lady," Billy said. "I could tell she convinced Art of one thing—he'll never sell Coke in here."

"Yeah! Wouldn't they do better if they toned down their hard sell?" Jack wanted to know. "Maybe start out by explaining their need to preserve their trademark; follow it up with enlisting your help, and maybe give you a six pack of Coke and a t-shirt, or something as incentive?"

"You guys are missing the point entirely," Pops chortled. "Hell, that lady wasn't from no Coca-Cola Company. It was an inside job. Pepsi sent her out to make sure their customers would never go over to the competition!" Adding, "I think you got played, Art."

Maybe he was right, but I had already written up the incident and mailed it to a local publication, who printed it.

A few days later a representative from Pepsi stopped in and dropped off a free case of soda and all sorts of party favors.

So I ask you, was she Coke...or was she Pepsi?

8. Exodus

*H*ave you been to my restaurant, *Arturo's Decent Italian Food*? If the place were a book, the censors would have closed it long ago due to its total lack of socially redeeming content.

You know the place. The one up there in Eastwood that looks like a throwback to the '20s that should have been thrown back to the Stone Age back in the '50s, which was when I set up shop there. From the outside it promises all the enticement and charm of a ghetto funeral home—but you have to cross the threshold before you can truly appreciate its total lack of ambiance.

Once people get inside and are able to savor the authentic (dilapidated) Old World (Neolithic) charm (dankness) of *Arturo's*, the compliments flow.

"When did Sloppy Joe's move from Utica?"

"I've been in slums with more class."

"I bet the menu has two items: *Dramamine* and *Rolaids!*"

There's one reason our business has grown by leaps and bounds: the tourist trade. Our customers simply cannot have Cousin Minerva or Aunt Jim-Bob come to Syracuse without bringing them to see Arturo's. (The out-of-towner is the one sporting an arm yanked from its socket.) For our regulars, telling their guests about *Arturo's*—even in the nauseating detail of an Arab curse—doesn't do the place justice. It simply has to be seen.

Sad to say, all of this is about to end. As a result of the afore-mentioned increase in business, we can no longer cut the mustard in the cramped quarters we now occupy. Did I say "cut" the mustard? Hell, our kitchen is so small we have to stick an elbow out the window just to open the jar!

Now, those are a couple of odd expressions—"cramped quarters" and "cut the mustard" (not to be confused with "cut the cheese"). One means "small living space" and the other means "up to snuff," which, oddly enough, is another odd expression.

Odd, like "oddly enough," itself. I wonder at what point one's oddly-ness qualifies as enough snuff to be up to?

"Hey, Art, still living in cramped quarters?"

"Oddly enough, yes, but it's on somebody else's dime..."

"Oh, I've had to stop on one of those before."

"...otherwise I wouldn't give a plugged nickel for it."

"So it isn't up to snuff?"

"Let's just say it doesn't cut the mustard."

"Fair enough."

Meanwhile back in Eastwood, it became apparent that Arturo's must go somewhere else—maybe you signed the petition. It was that three part one: "Stop Cuba from sending Criminals to the U.S.; Bring back the Death Penalty, and; Get Arturo's out of Eastwood!"

Starr and I looked high and low; then we got high and looked lower, but no place we could afford would have us. Then we saw the old Mancini's in Mattydale—it even had the plentiful parking and spacious kitchen we so desperately needed. And so...

Arturo's is moving to Mattydale!

Lest you fear we'll lose our quaintness (squalor), rest assured: we will be taking our wacky menu, our wackier signs and our wackiest staff along with us. So come see us in Mattydale—and don't forget to bring your sweet Aunt Jim-Bob!

9. School Organs

Throughout the land, a great hullabaloo has risen over high school students' right to a free press. Well, if pro basketball players have the right to press whenever they please, then why shouldn't high school students? (You're right. I'm ashamed. That was just too corny.)

Seriously though, as the literati among us know, the issue is this: should students have the right to express themselves in their school organ, free from editorial control? My answer is, "I don't understand the question."

You see, I went to a parochial senior high school. The total population was 62 students (63 on those rare days when Crazy Max Malloy wasn't suspended or expelled—*and* deigned to show up.) Our school was so small, we didn't just lack a school organ— we couldn't even afford to have the piano tuned! (Knock it off, Art.)

And ours was one of the more fortunate "nun-schools"; *we* actually had a science lab. Not the assembly hall or lunchroom converted into a temporary lab like the other schools, but a room dedicated completely to science, with not one, but *two* lab tables. Each table was equipped with its own Bunsen burner, unusable, with gas lines so old they were cracked, and a sink fed by a water hose whose off-and-on valve was way in the back of the boiler room. We were taken there once to dissect a frog (to the lab, not the boiler room). Fourteen students, each with a scalpel, and a frog. Not one frog *each*, mind you—just one lonely little amphibian for all of us, trapped in a scene of terror that would have made Kermit drop a toadstool in horror, if he'd been born yet.

Despite having such an advanced science lab, our school wasn't all that progressive. Students today want freedom of expression? Hell, we weren't even allowed freedom of thought! "*Master Belge,*" Sister Mary Crotchety would say. (They called everyone 'master' back then, except the girls, of course—and oh, yes: my buddy Tom Baytes. For some reason, he was called "Mister.") "Master *Belge*, wipe that smile off your face; I know what you are thinking."

Which was embarrassing, because at that age my usual thoughts were along the lines of, "Can you really see up a girl's dress if she's wearing patent leather shoes? How many times do you have to kiss a girl before you're entitled to take a shot at second base? And what if a girl finally lets me do IT someday, and suddenly her father comes home and we get hung-up like copulating dogs occasionally do, because everyone says that really happened to someone they know?"

Anyway, "freedom" was not a word in the nun-nicular vocabulary.

But seriously, why should students be granted "freedom of the press" when no other writers have it? I mean, sure, every editor tells his reporters that they have carte blanche, until they write something the overpaid-blue-pencil-pusher doesn't like. Then they're told it's against "community spirit" or "editorial policy," or that it's "in bad taste" or "of no interest to our readers." All of this BS is really just different ways of saying "It won't sell." So if the writer can't read between the lines (chortle, snicker) he finds his article castrated and buried. No, really, a writer has no control over his own material. Check it out for yourself. In the paragraph before the last paragraph, was the part about the go-go dancer playing Hide the Python still there? Mm-hmm, I thought not. And what page does this article appear on? Certainly not page one. See? Just like I said: castrated and buried by money-centric editors.

No, these school kids don't need to worry about the illusory freedom of the press. They need to learn the harsh reality of the *true* Golden Rule: He who has the gold, rules.

10. Guns Don't Kill Killers; People Do

If you don't believe the title, go check Gary Gilmore's headstone. I'll wait.

Okay, then. Now that you're back, you can forget the title of this article and its opening sentence. They have piddly little to do with what I want to talk about. It's just that the title kinda sorta tumbled out of my mind—a mind that is otherwise built like a steel trap—and appeared to be just the catchy phrase needed to lure readers to read a treatise that otherwise would have had all of the appeal of dancing nude at the Alamogordo Nuclear Testing Site in the late summer of 1945.

Just so you understand where I'm coming from, I want to talk about guns, not the death penalty. If I did want to talk about the death penalty, I'd ask you to consider that many people believe that keeping a person on death row for years while umpteen appeals are made is cruel and unusual punishment. On the other hand, there are those who believe that the death penalty itself is cruel and unusual. These folks naturally believe that every appeal should be allowed, even if they take years and cost millions.

But like I said, I don't want to talk about that. I want to talk about guns.

The thing that I have most against guns is that they scare me. Years ago, Arturo's was held up by an armed robber. My number four daughter, who was the prime robbee (robberee? robbery-ee?) calmly described the gunman and his apparel to the police. I remember clearly thinking how unclearly I'd be thinking if I were she. "Yes, officer," I'd say, "I can give you a description. It was made of metal and had a round hole in the end that was pointed right at the outside of my head, while the inside of my head kept shouting to itself, '*It's a gun! Oh my god, it's a gun!*'"

I suppose there are people who aren't scared of guns. There are probably people who aren't scared of the dark, either; I just don't happen to be one of them. I'm also deathly afraid of death, jail, Khadafi and peanut butter ice cream. Each of us has our own boogiemen.

I remember an incident that occurred in the early fifties when I was attending Albany State. I was bantering with Jack, a fellow student and friend who happened to be Black. We were jokingly trading racial slurs when something he said maligned white bravado. I retorted that "whitey" knew that all he had to do was show "blacky" a little of "blacky's" own blood and the fight went out of him. Jack immediately retorted that once "whitey" saw the glint of steel, all you saw of him was ass and elbows. I don't know if I was right about Blacks and blood, but he had *me* pegged with that glint of steel bit.

Then again, I wasn't too bright, verbally tangling with this dude who regularly out-bull-jived professors of education, who are noted throughout academia as being the bull-jiviest of all professors. We used to marvel how Jack, when seemingly backed into a corner by a prof, would start spouting statistics that proved his point. And he would back up his stats by naming the Midwestern University where the study was done, and even the name of the professor who conducted it. For instance, he once cited statistics from "Knox College's Analysis of Etymological Transitions of Common Usage," by Dr. Keith Goldhammer. What made his citations even more marvelous was that there were precious few facts to be found among them: except for the name of the University, he had made the whole thing up—title, professor, statistics and all. But didn't the Goldhammer thingy sound like an honest-to-God study to you? It did to our professors. In the two years we went to school together, not one of them ever challenged one of Jack's scholarly citations.

Nevertheless, Jack was right about me: show me a gun and I'll show me the door.

Now, about the "right to bear arms" brouhaha: the people who insist on maintaining their constitutional right are saying, "I have that right, period. I don't need to explain why; I just don't want to lose it." It seems to me that they don't want to explain because their explanation would expose their paranoia: "Someday the government is going to come after me, and I want to be sure I have a gun handy when they do." That certainly is a paranoid belief, but in today's world, a case could be made that it's a valid, *intelligent* paranoid belief.

The problem is that if the government *does* decide to come after them in the not-so-far apocalyptic future, it won't be coming with rifles. No, the government will be bringing nuclear arms—because by then, "ordinary citizens" will have *bazookas*. We're talking really big nuclear arms, here: Sumo wrestler arms, with weight-lifter abs and no neck, mounted on massive mobile missile silos.

But that doesn't scare me. Not anymore. Not since I started living in this fallout shelter. I just hope I don't run out of light bulbs...

11. In God We Trust

Have you ever read your money, beyond checking the denomination? Go ahead, pull a bill from your pocket. Read it closely. You'll notice it's stamped *Federal Reserve Note*. If you're lucky, it will also say *$100*, but if you're like me, you just borrowed five bucks from your son.

Here's the tricky part: no matter the denomination, that bill does not say it's actually worth anything. The only assurance you have is the vague statement that "This note is legal tender for all debts public and private." Which I translate as "not worth more than the paper it's printed on, but everybody has to accept it anyway."

I once came into possession of four, one-dollar silver notes. "Art," I said to myself. "This ain't your everyday monopoly money!" I knew they must be valuable because it said right on them, "This certifies that there is on deposit in the Treasury of the United States of America one dollar in silver payable to the bearer on demand." Well, all right! Four dollars in silver, mine for the asking.

I asked.

"No!" the man at the Treasury Department said. He didn't have my silver, but he suggested that I try the Federal Reserve. I didn't know who they were. I know a lot of guys in the Army Reserve. Maybe the Federal Reserve is made up of extra bureaucrats ready to replace fallen members of Congress. In any event, I did find them listed, so I gave them a call.

"No!" They didn't have my silver either.

"Well what can I do with these silver certificate dollar notes, then?" I asked before thinking.

"Bring them in and we'll give you Federal Reserve notes for them," he replied.

"No!" I said. Gee whiz, I didn't just fall off the Brinks truck yesterday. What kind of fool does he think I am—that I would trade in my silver backed semolians for his hot-air buckaroos? Besides, I saw a picture of the Federal Reserve vault in the Encyclopedia Americana, and it was loaded with *gold bullion*. All I was asking for was the crummy silver I was entitled to, not their precious gold. Another thing he didn't know I knew; the Federal Reserve backs its money with promissory government notes—and we all know how noteworthy our government's promises are. Just ask the Apache or the Iroquois.

He suggested that I call a coin collector. I did so.

I could tell that she was on the edge of her seat, squeezing the phone, she was so excited. Now I had something.

"Are they new-looking?" she panted. "Uncirculated?"

I had to admit that the clap and the plague combined had been passed around less virulently than these bad boys had. I could hear the drool on her lip crackle as it dried. She suggested I try the U.S. Mint.

That's it! That's where my silver had to be. The Mint has vaults of the stuff at West Point.

"Sorry, Charlie," said the mint man with a chuckle, "but if you'll bring them in, I'll give you some shiny, new, silver quarters for 'em."

Well, really! We all know that absolutely, positively guaranteed, there is not going to be the least trace of silver in those solder suckers.

And that was that.

As time went by, I lost track of those special singles. Probably stuffed them in a charity box or a g-string somewhere along the line.

And it's true, I didn't get any silver, but it could be worse. Those four irredeemable dollars redeemed my faith in the way my country works, or rather, the way it doesn't.

12. That Costs Extra

We are smack in the middle of the no-frills era, which is doublespeak for "We used to do that for our customers as part of our regular service, but the term 'regular service' has been shelved as archaic by the Organization of Manufacturers, Retailers and Washing Machine Repairmen." It is a pleasant surprise today—an innovation, even—when we find a company like the local grocery chain whose employees actually help you to your car with your purchases.

On the national level, probably the greatest innovator in the service area has to be Ma Bell: she's always breaking up old services—and charging new fees for them.

Ma will gladly install a phone for you, with no charge for installation. Why? Because it's been replaced by several "lesser charges."

"What's that, Sir? You don't want to answer it in the attic? But that's where the line enters the house. What you do with it after that is up to you. If you'd like us to extend it from the attic into the living area, that will involve wiring, for which we charge ninety cents per month, for as long as we both shall live.

"A cord? But sir, we supplied you with a cord. Oh, I see; your wife says four inches isn't long enough." (She's always saying that.) "Yes we can fix that. Longer cords come in two sizes: ninety-five cents and $1.25 per month, for as long as we both shall live."

Would you rather have a chime instead of a bell? Easy to remember number? Gladly, for $72 dollars per annum in perpetuity, amen.

Speed dial? No problem. You push a single button and watch how speedily they dial up the charges on your bill, even though it takes just as long as if you dialed it yourself. Conference calls? Call forwarding? Call waiting? A flashing light when the phone rings? A Mickey Mouse phone? Nostalgia phone? Nausea phone? They're all available, at an extra monthly charge, for as long as we both shall live. I do.

But the telephone company's greatest contribution to business practices is not the invention of services; it's the un-invention of them, thereby charging customers for getting (and later, for not getting) services they never wanted in the first place. The new 900 numbers are a good example.

With 900 numbers, businesses can charge you whatever they want while you attempt to indulge your fantasies. On the other hand, if you're willing to pay ten dollars, the telephone company will castrate (or spay) your phone, so all 900 numbers are neutered. I didn't ask for "Love Connection," "Date Line," or "Confessions." Did you? So why do we have to cough up a ten spot that we busted our cajones to earn, to not get something we never asked for to begin with?

I investigated this recently and was told by a Bell representative that for my ten dollars, not only 900 numbers, but 740's, 770's, 820's, 960's and a slew of others would also be blocked. I asked what services those numbers were for. The rep had no idea, but whatever they were, she said in a cheery voice, I wouldn't have to worry about them. Kind of makes you wonder what Ma has in store, don't it?

I feel trite mentioning the most famous un-invention, the extra charge for not having your name and number printed, so that people you don't know won't be able to call you. Beats the hell out of the planned obsolescence we ranted about in the fifties, doesn't it?

There are more.

First, she invented the long-distance call charge. Then she invented the 800 number, so that businesses could pay her oodles not to charge for long distance calls. Ma, I'm sure, feels no regrets over the fact that while the Post Office was going from a zone charging system to a blanket fee for delivery within our national borders, she was doing the opposite. Can it possibly cost several dollars per minute for the smidgen of electricity necessary to send a voice cross-country? Well, perhaps she has one regret: not for charging for long-distance in the first place, but for taking so long to invent the 800 number to un-charge for it.

What I'm waiting for is the No-Solicitors-Can-Call-You blocking service. (Editor's note: How prophetic!) Or better yet, the Computerized-Soliciting-Machines-Will-Receive-A-Zillion-Volts-Feedback service.

Uh, oh! What if the US Postal Service takes a yellow page from the phone company's book and starts charging us to not receive junk mail? It would be like a reverse stamp tax. And the people? We'd be licked.

The other day, I made a collect call that was handled by a computer. I had to tell the computer my name, which it recorded. I assume it was spewed back to the person about to answer the phone.

That got me thinking.

Every tavern gets a million phone calls for customers. For an extra charge, the phone company could install an automatic loud speaker-pager. But that's not where the real money is—the real money is in the *non-service*. At least half the people in any given tavern at any given time, don't want to be found. They are the lazy, shiftless, good-for-nothing shirkers of the world...you know, husbands. These anonymity seekers would pay a dollar to punch in their number when they stumble in. The phone would automatically answer any calls for them with, "Sorry, there is no one here answering to that number. Would you like to try another? For an arm and a leg we will gladly connect you."

Now, *that's* a non-service I'd be willing to pay for.

13. Bettors Weepers, Losers Keepers

A s Abe Lincoln once meant to say, "All of the people screw up some of the time, and some of the people screw up all of the time." Or, as Dr. C. Curien Smith, my most outstanding teacher, once put it, "If you want to know which way a river is going to run tomorrow, find out which way it has run in the past." What am I trying to say? That some people and some projects are patent losers, and you can make money betting against them, if you can find the proverbial unparted fool.

I remember when I was in college there was one guy who never—not in four years—told a joke without screwing it up. I can still hear him saying, "...and the train conductor shouts in a thick southern drawl, 'No'folk, Virginia!' Oh, wait—did I tell you that the girl's name was Virginia? I knew I forgot something. Here, let me start again..."

Niagara Mohawk Electric (Ni-Mo) is certainly way ahead in this field. Those guys have turned losing into an art form. They could fall into a river of rosewater and come out smelling like doggy-doo. Several years ago, my stockbroker talked me into buying options whose value depended upon the successful start up of the new Ni-Mo puke-ular power plant—a start-up that was scheduled several days hence. This was only their seven hundred and seventy second try to get their abominable reactor to work without leaking in so many places even the government couldn't hide it.

If only I had said to myself, "Look at the way the No'folk River runs, Virginia," maybe I wouldn't have been so stupid. The half of my brain that wasn't besotted with alcohol should have made me say, "I want to get into those options, but only if you'll sell them short for me." But I didn't say that. I bought the stocks as is, the reactor didn't react well, and neither did the shares on the market.

I lost a bundle.

There it was, my golden opportunity to bet on a loser as a loser—and, well, I guess I did just that. I just hadn't figured on the prowess of the second professional loser in the game, namely, me. And now you know why I never give anyone a piece of my mind: the supply is far too limited.

I did learn a valuable lesson, however. Just because I was stupid does not mean there's no "sure money" to be made in the market. There is, but it accrues to the investment firms. Whether you and I make a killing, cut our losses or lose it all, Mister Schwaab gets his glob. Brokerage firms, my unfirm fanny! They don't go broke—they get rich by betting *our* money.

"Brokerage" just refers to what they do to the rest of us.

Speaking of betting on losers, beating up on our mayor's latest monumental erection is in vogue now. He's building the Carousel Mall, a.k.a. the Cancer Cell Mall or the Scare-us-all Mall, on the shores of Gitchi-Gloomy a.k.a. Onondaga Lake, a.k.a. one of the most contaminated lakes on Earth. Xaviera Hollander has a better shot at being purified. If they drained the lake and dredged eight feet of dirt from the bottom it might be pure—but only until the next rainfall leached even more poison from beneath the surrounding industrial plants back into it.

And the cost of the mall—wasted environment aside—by the most conservative estimates is so staggering as to set the minds of everyone reeling—except the mind of Mario, our prodigal gub'ner.

Speaking of chronic losers, how many shots are we going to give Mario to bankrupt the state? He definitely needs another term to really get things wrong, and being the loser-lovers we are, I'm sure we'll give it to him. Proving once again that when a *regular person* goes insane, we send him to an asylum; when a politician goes insane, we send him to the Capitol.

And we'll do it, again and again and again. And we'll lose, again and again and again. And thus it ever shall be, forever and ever, amen.

You can bet on it.

14. Infernal Revenue

Years ago I read an article on legitimate, but little known ways to cut your tax bill. The author stated that restaurateurs who often bought provisions in supermarkets could deduct the cost of their local newspaper if they used it to check for sales and coupons. Made sense to me. If you purchase something as a research tool that's going to increase your profit, it should be allowed as a business expense.

So I called Infernal Retinue and had this conversation:

"I understand that if I use the local newspaper to help me make a profit in my business, I am entitled to write off the subscription price as a legitimate expense."

"Why should you? I can't, and I work for the IRS."

"I'm sorry to hear that, but I wasn't asking for you, I was asking for me. I'm assuming you're not in business, and I am."

"Who do you think you are, somebody special, just because you have a business?"

I put on my suavest voice, hoping to smooth the feathers of this ruffled grouse. "We seem to be getting off the track here. I really just want an official ruling on whether or not the paper is, for me, a proper deduction."

"*You're* off the track; you're also stupid. I gave you your answer already—No!"

"I can't accept that. Please connect me with your supervisor. I want a ruling from someone of higher authority."

"No!"

"What is your name?"

"I'm not telling you that, either."

Click. Bzzzzzz.

Dial.

Misdial.

Furious redial.

"Internal Revenue Service."

"I would like to speak to a supervisor, please."

A new voice came on the line. "Can I help you?"

"Yes. I was very rudely treated by one of your information clerks, who even refused to give me her name. I want to report her."

"Certainly, sir. I'll take that report for you. Now, what was her name?"

As I hung up, it occurred to me that the time I spent arguing with the IRS ought to be legitimate tax deduction, but I'll be damned if I'm going to call and ask.

15. Green Grows the Tarmac

I'm one of the most adept people around the house in the whole history of adept people around the house.

I built a doll house with so much lumber in it, it took a crane to get it into my granddaughter's attic, where it will remain in pristine condition for years to come. I crafted cabinets for our kitchen, which inspired the design for the common orange crate. I still get royalties from that one. And house painting is a snap, I completed the entire outside of my house in just under five years.

Plumber, electrician, mason; pick a trade, any trade—that's my muddle name.

Last spring I turned my Zen-like concentration on my lawn. Having faith in my own prodigious abilities, I planned my attack. I would read up on the subject, buy the necessary supplies and tools, and then—look out, lawn!

The first book I read taught me about horticultural shock, which is exactly what hit me when I realized that the author was talking about hard physical labor like shoveling, raking and hoeing. I decided I didn't know enough yet, and that more reading was called for. I started reading the yellow pages, newspaper ads, shopper's guides, that sort of thing.

Eventually I found what I was looking for: a prestigious firm that oozed expertise. You could see it written all over their ad, *Only $29.95 for the Average Lawn*. I figured I could get an even better deal, since my lawn was definitely below average. So I called to set up an appointment. "First thing in the morning," they said.

When they didn't show up first, middle, or even last thing in the morning, I called another prestigious firm. When *they* didn't show up, I made a date with a third one.

When the expert finally did show up, he said, "You don't need a lawn doctor; you need a witch doctor. What've you been treating your lawn with, Agent Orange? If I were you, I would start from the bottom up—with a *backhoe!*" Laughing, he shook his head and left.

I called still another outfit. Their man told me that he could save my lawn. Oh frumptious joy, I wouldn't have to shovel and rake till I got as hunch-backed as Quasimodo. I pictured myself swinging on a rope up into a cathedral with a beautiful gypsy girl under my arm, while I shouted, "Sanctuary!" Cool scene, man, just so long as I didn't have to look like Charles Laughton. The expert said he would apply something he called *10-20-10 with Weed Killer.*

I wondered what 10-20-10 was—Minnie Mouse's measurements, maybe? But if it could save my lawn, I'd go for it. The catch was that I'd have to water the lawn regularly, and rake it as well. The raking, he said, was very important, because vermin would hide under the leaves and stuff, squinched down in the lawn.

What could be down there, I wondered? Grubs looking for a stake? Carpenter ants building a tiny cathedral? Weevils searching for a boll-full?

Could I never grow cotton on this land again?

I didn't realize how successful my lawn care program was until winter set in. Way back in the spring I didn't think I had an outside chance of growing a lawn. But apparently, I did stand just such a chance, because that's what I got—an outside lawn. The middle was void of any hint of green, but there were six inches of grass around the perimeter, growing like crazy and spilling onto the driveway and sidewalks. The damn thing looked like Friar Tuck's tonsured head.

And I knew that when winter hit, that grass would form a speed bump under the snow, and I'd be stubbing my snow shovel on it and breaking my freakin' arm.

Eureka! That gives me an idea: why not make the *whole damn thing* a speed bump? Next year, I'm going to have an asphalt company lay six inches of tar over my whole lawn and paint the whole thing green. Then I'll sit back and laugh and laugh and laugh, as spring rolls around again and I watch the grass not grow, on my decidedly not-average lawn.

The neighbors will no doubt be jaded with envy over my superior gardening skills. Hey, what can I say? I guess I do have a green thumb, after all. Wanna see? Here, lemme pull it outta my...

16. I Didn't Learn Squat in Kindergarten

Robert Fulghum wrote *Everything I Need to Know I Learned in Kindergarten*. To which I respond, "Robert Fulgham is a poopy-head!"

Because what I've learned *since* kindergarten is this: until you understand how to apply what you've learned, you ain't learned diddly. In other words, what counts is what you learn after you know it all. It's fine and dandy to know that the shortest distance between two points is a straight line, but when you've just loved thy neighbor and her husband is coming in the front door, you'll get home quicker—and in fewer pieces—if experience has taught you that desertion is the better part of valor. If you've learned that, you'll know to take a serpentine, circuitous exit—out the window, say, or around the back.

Let's examine some of the tenets of this syrupy sweet, new kinderfaith:

"Put Things Back Where You Found Them"

It isn't always that simple. What things? Whose things? Where did you find them, and under what circumstances? Maybe the thing you found doesn't belong where you found it. If it's something *I* put there, there's a good chance it doesn't. Or maybe it does belong where you found it, but it belongs to someone else. Did you steal it? Did you steal it from a very big person? (If that's the case, returning it might put you in more danger than keeping it.) Did you find it on the street? Was it a hundred dollar bill? (Was it green and white with a picture of a President on it? Thanks—I thought I lost that!) Or maybe you found a Rolex, or a bag of cash. By all means, you should put it back and hope that the rightful owner returns to claim it. (You should also maybe crack coconuts with your forehead.)

"Take a Nap in the Afternoon"

Want to try that one on your boss? Even Samuel Gompers

and John L. Lewis didn't try for that one. Take a nap, yeah right! Some of us *work* for a living. Reminds me of an old cartoon: an office drone is sacked out at his desk, when the boss walks in and barks, *"Why aren't you working?!"* Replies the drone, "I didn't hear you coming!"

"Share Everything"

Sounds pretty avant garde. I wonder if we could interest Poland, Czechoslovakia, Lithuania, and Latvia in this revolutionary theory. It always seems that the mighty share the champagne and caviar, while the meek (to paraphrase Mordred) inherit the dirt.

"Don't Hit People"

Can we redefine "people" to exclude Hitler, Stalin, Charles Manson, and his brother Marilyn?

"Say You're Sorry When You Hurt Someone"

Not if that someone is Hitler or Stalin or either of the Mansons. (Or Hulk Hogan; he's always so grumpy.)

"Flush"

Okay, I gotta go along with this one. But I think Fulgham wimped out by his failure to address a serious wrong done to boys and men: the insistence that we lift the seat before we take a leak, then lower it when we're done.

I know what the distaff half of you are going to say, so don't trouble yourselves. To the *dikstaff* half of you, I say, who says? Who *says* the rule is "put the seat down"? Women—that's who! Do they put it up for our benefit when they're done? It seems only fair.

But every woman I've said this to has looked at me like I was more full of shite than an Equatorial dung beetle. And when I said it to *Starr*, she replied, "Tell ya what: You leave that seat up in the middle of the night one more time, and you'll be wearing the friggin' thing for a necklace!"

I may have to re-think my position on this one.

"Don't Spit into the Wind"

This is one that Fulgham didn't list, but should have. Maybe he was a late bloomer, and didn't master the finer facts of phlegm phlinging until later.

I could go on and on (as you well know), but I just heard a splash and a scream coming from the bathroom. Experience tells me that the straightest line between myself and safety would be a serpentine one. Out the window, say, or around the back...

17. Sweepstakes Shoo-in

The next time you see those TV ads for the magazine lottery—you know, the ones where the prize-mobile drives up, several suits get out and jam into the foyer to bring the good news that the resident has won the ten million dollar super prize—take a good look at the winners and you'll notice a common denominator: They all think "Golden Girls" is the adult version of "Baywatch." (Okay, maybe that's a poor example. If the women of "Baywatch" said the things that the "Golden Girls" say, the Falwells of our country would be leading a torchlight parade to their beach à la Frankenstein's mob.) What I'm trying to say is that the winners are always of such supernumerariority that they spell old, "olde."

Just imagine that you're a seventy-two-year-olde widow who has recently mortgaged your once-upon-a-time free-of-debt home to save your no-goodnik son's hide for the umpteenth time. You're just sitting down, finally, to enjoy a night's television, when klieg lights glare through your windows. You answer the pounding on your front door and get crowded back into the house by an invasion of the aforementioned suits. The dinner you just ate threatens to make a fast exit south. You're fumbling in your pockets for your nitro tablets when one of the suits screams, "Congratulations! You've just won ten million dollars!"

Quick! What do you do?

You clutch your chest, follow your lunch to the floor, and cross over into Beulah Land, that's what.

And that is just the way they plan it to go.

You see, they have three payment options for you to choose from: monthly, quarterly or annually. You notice that none of those choices is one very, very big one, up front, right now. Au contrare, olde frere. A little simple math tells you that you're going to have to live thirty more years to collect all of that ten mil. (And whichever option you choose, you'll notice upon reading over the glossy brochures, nowhere do they state whether you will be paid at the end or beginning of the month, quarter or year.) So to be on the safe side we all choose monthly, saying to ourselves, "Heck! I could be dead in three months or a year." Little do we know how true that is. And little do we know, how well they know how true that is.

It's no mistake that Ed McMahon and Dick Clark's pictures appear in the ads. They're subtly trying to convince you that no one ever ages or dies, just like these two geezers who are beating their three score years and ten with very short sticks.

There are two reasons for this strategy. The more geezers in play, the more likely a geezer will win. And having a geezer win increases the likelihood that the winner will die well before most of the prize money has been paid out.

Now that I know this I've contrived to stack the odds in my favor. Whenever I send in an entry, I write at the top in red ink, "Please notify me immediately if I am a winner because I am a diabetic, anorexic, coronary-occluded, high-risk cancer profile, accident prone, alcoholic, former coal-mining and asbestos working octogenarian, who would like to use what little time I have left enjoying my sweepstakes winnings."

The signature I append would make chicken scratches look like expert calligraphy.

I expect to hear from them soon. In the meantime, where are my nitro pills?

18. It's a Dog's Life

Woof! Who doesn't understand "woof"? It's pretty straight-forward. Certainly much manlier than the wimpy "arf" that Little Orphan Annie's dog Sandy utters. And it's ten times more macho than "bow-wow." I mean, how un-macho can a bark be? In dog circles, even "meow" is taken more seriously than "bow-wow."

"Think about it, Art," you admonish. "No animal actually utters any of those sounds. They're what linguists call onomato-poeic—words that sound like the actual sounds they define. Have you ever seen a dog put her lips together and say 'bow-wow' or 'arf' or 'woof'? Of course not, because dogs don't have lips! The best you're going to get is 'ow-ow' and 'oo'."

To answer your question: no, I've never seen (or heard) a dog say bow-wow or arf, but woof is another story. My wife's best friend's best friend is a bull mastiff named Courtney who says woof all the time—unmistakably, undeniably as clearly as Julie Andrews enunciates lyrics. And now, catch this—Starr's best friend has also taught this bull mastiff to meow. Yes, Courtney actually says me-ow. We are obviously dealing with a bilingual canine here.

But there's a big difference between a cat and a bull mastiff, so when Courtney says "woof!" it's with all the bombast of a marine drill instructor bellowing orders from the bottom of an empty 50,000 gallon drum.

Let me more fully describe the bull mastiff to you, in case you never want to see one—they're built like a reverse iceberg. Whereas the ice iceberg has seven-eighths of its weight in its bottom quarters, this animal has seven-eighths of its weight in its head quarters. Imagine a face slightly less sweet and gentle than Freddie Krueger's, and you'll have a good mental picture of the grotesquery of a bull mastiff. It defies being caricatured, because it already is a caricature.

However, looks, like sounds, can be deceiving. To the not-so-casual observer, Courtney's "woof" sounds like "Move an inch and I'll bite off your leg!" But what she's really saying is, "I don't know you, so scratch my head, or better yet, give me a treat, and I'll show you my greatest trick: falling asleep in your lap in a puddle of my own drool."

She has other peccadilloes, too. Take her for a walk and you'll find that she'll obey the command to heel—as long as you know how she interprets that word. To her, it means the same thing as saying to a pro football player that the no-clipping rule has been abolished. You learn quickly that you never holler "heel" at Courtney when walking country roads with any oncoming traffic.

She obeys other commands too, like sit, stay, and come— every bit as promptly as a sulky twelve-year-old being told it's time to go to bed. Just fast enough to avoid punishment, but with an attitude that says, "I'm gonna do it as slowly and loudly as I can, just to piss you off."

Maybe you think I'm giving her too much credit (the dog, not the child). "Art, you poodle brain," you're thinking. "Dogs don't cogitate like we do!" Well, then, tell me what you think of this little trick of hers. Late in the evening, Courtney will go to the door and bark, her signal to her mistress that nature calls. But every now and then, as her mistress reaches for the door handle, Courtney will do a quick about-face and run to the couch and jump into the spot formerly occupied by her owner. Once ensconced, she fights all attempts to dislodge her, looking for all the world as though she's thinking, "Kind of stupid of you to give up this nice warm spot, but I'm not dumb enough to make the same mistake."

Courtney has one fault—she's scared poopless of anything in the air. Hearing an airplane makes her stick her head under a bed, leaving her torso exposed in an if-I-can't-see-you-then-you-can't-see-me approach to problem-solving. Arriving at a hot-air balloon exhibition she hunkered down beneath the steering wheel as soon as the driver vacated his position. It took thirty minutes to get her dislodged. Spotting a dirigible, she crammed herself under a wooden chair and closed her eyes.

It raises the question of why we humans keep and love such obviously devious and useless pets, unwilling to follow the simplest of commands.

Woof! Gotta go! I hear Starr rattling my dinner bowl.

19. Piece of Cake

My doctor said, "I'm going to need an MRI to really assess the damage you've done to your shoulder. Take this paper down to the second floor. Wait for the results and bring the report to me."

You see, I have an affliction that is deadly. My ear canals, my eyesight, my muscular control, and my sense of my balance have all teamed up to make me as secure as the shed our daughter Sandra built in our back yard when she was six.

You probably think I'm exaggerating, but the primary cause of death among the elderly is falling.

We trip, slip or flip and end up on our kiesters—and consequently enjoy a stay in Hope Memorial. Hospitals are oversized petrie dishes teeming with bacteria and viruses (virusii? virii?), to which we persons of a reasonable age are especially vulnerable. So we contract pneumonia, or hepatitis or some other damn thing, and the prime cause of death is listed as that ailment, not the fall—just like in the Old Testament, it's the fall that does us in.

I have fallen ten times so far this year. Death wish, you think? The one I'm writing about occurred on the granite stairs at a friend's house. The last step blended in with the flooring, so you were stepping on an optical illusion. Optical illusions are not load-rated, but I am. Did you know that granite is harder than marble? I didn't, but I do.

On my way down in the elevator, I wondered what "MRI" stood for. And then I saw the infernal machine, and immediately knew that anything that scared me that much just by one glance did not portend serenity for my proximate future. I mean, did he actually intend to squeeze me into that tubey microwavey thingy? And then what—bake me like a cake?

"Are you nervous?" the attendant asked. "No, no," I squeaked, sounding like the Tin Man needing an oil change.

"That's fine, Mr. Arturo. And are you a claustrophobic?"

What does religion have to do with this—was he suggesting a need for prayer? I just shook my head no. Damned if I was going to let him know that I could be just a teensy-weensy bit scared. But I did have one question.

"Does that thing open wider than that? Like now it's set for children, right?"

"Nope," he said. "That's it right there."

"Well, how do I turn over in that thing?"

"You don't," he said. "Hop up."

I hopped up and he fed me into the maw of the beast. I tried to say that I had just remembered an important meeting across town, but all that came out of my mouth were pitiful squeaks.

Trapped inside this modern medical miracle, I was assaulted by horrible grinding, scraping, pounding noises. In a flash of warm, wet insight, I knew what "MRI" stood for—*Machine Related Incontinence*. It sounded like someone was whaling away at the outside of the thing with a sledge hammer. Then it got quiet. I suspected a malfunction.

A few seconds later, the technician slid me out of the tube, confirming my suspicions.

"You did very well Mr. Arturo. You didn't move so much as a finger for the whole half-hour you were in there."

Half-hour? It seems like a minute or two, tops. I must have passed out, but I'd be damned if I was going to admit that for the last twenty-eight minutes I was out cold.

"Nothing to it, Son, piece of cake!"

20. Letter to My Son

*D*ear Son,
    There are many parents in the land who want their children to have all of the things they never had. I don't know how you feel about that philosophy, but as for me, I never fell for that crapola. I always put first things first: beer in the fridge, bread in the box, and money to pay the Saturday baby-sitter, in that order. These were followed by mortgage payments, electric payments, and Ma Bell. Everything else was catch as catch can.

Over the years, you had your share of requests. Do you remember asking for:
1. A skateboard? (age 5)
2. A set of Jarts? (age 7)
3. A bike? (age 12)
4. A car? (age 18)
5. A visit with my girlfriend?

And I answered...
1. So you can kill yourself?
2. So you can kill everyone else in the neighborhood?
3. Every time you cross the street, I hold my breath because you don't look, and now you want to ride a machine in the middle of it?
4. Sounds good. How much have you got saved for the insurance?
5. For God's sake, Son, keep your voice down; your mother's right in the kitchen. Maybe we could put your car on my policy.

To help you out as you go through life, here are four principles that my philosophy is built on:

Turnabout is Fair Play: How well I remember my dad, who couldn't afford to give me those things either, putting his hand on my shoulder, saying, "Get a job."

Right of Inheritance: Not only couldn't my father afford them, but his father, and his father's father before him, couldn't either.

First Come, First Served: I was born long before you.

The Sacred Right to Possess Personal Property: Which means that everybody better keep their hands off my returnable cans and bottles. When I'm short of cash, I use them to get a six pack.

Now that you are grown and have a son of your own, I hope you realize the wisdom with which I raised you. Don't try to give your child everything while you go without. You work hard and deserve a few cans of beer out of this life, too.

Love,
Dad

P.S. Sears is having a sale on ten speeds, and while it's not your son's birthday or anything, it is summer. And I happen to have some money I was saving for a new bowling ball, but I can bowl just as badly with an alley ball. (Ha! Ha!) Plus, now that I'm retired, I've got the time to teach him. Besides I really haven't bought him anything since the sled last winter. We can't count the cart last month, since I got it so cheap at that auction. So if you don't mind, it would please me to get it for him, after all, you're only young once.

Oh yah, tell him I haven't forgotten—I'm still looking for that bow and arrow set I promised him. After all, son, I want your children to have all of the things I never had...

21. Love Letter

I've got this friend who is not averse to pulling a practical joke now and then. And he's *good* at it. He never uses the same ruse twice.

He once called and said that he had a flat and needed a ride because his spare was also flat. When I found his truck the tires were just fine and dandy. Then I noticed the truck was parked in front of a bar, and went inside to find him sucking beer through his shite-eating grin.

After a drink or three, I told him I was ready to go.

"Oh no, you're not!" He replied.

"And why izzat?" I asked.

"Cuz I borrowed your keys while you were inna can an' they assa...assadenally slipped into the ice machine. You'll hafta unplug it and wait until they thaw!"

Nice guy. Good friend. I silently vowed my revenge.

A few weeks later I, um, assadenally found a magazine advertising an array of sex toys, and had a great idea: a practical joke with a punch line that he, of all people, would really appreciate.

First, I typed a letter:

Dearest Billy,

I hope you still remember me I was in a bar with a frend and you walk in with your frends and we wwas having a good time but you notissed I cant handle my drinks and you finished my drinks when no one was loking.

You was such a gentleman and I was realy impresed and I hopped you would ask me for a date and when you said I'll give you a ride I was saying to myself well its about time and when we got to my apartment I kept dropping my keys and you oppened the door and you sed you would luv to com in but after the drinks you had plus mine you was to blitssed blizzed and I was two so you kissed me on the fourhead and said goodnight sweetie and left.

Do you remember when I told you I was gonna be a model well guess what? I got a job in a magazine!!!!! My picture is on page 64!!!! I will lok you up next time Im in town.

Luv,

Bambi

I mailed the letter and the magazine to Billy's house and waited for the fun to begin.

As luck would have it Billy's wife picked up the mail the day the package came. She tried to resist, but her curiosity got the better of her.

She read the letter.

She blew her stack.

They fought all night.

Finally, Billy called me. I swore I had nothing to do with it. I hung up and laughed my buns off.

He called again and he begged me to tell his wife, insisting that the letter had to have come from me, despite the misspellings and poor grammar.

I told him to put his wife on the phone and asked her if she had looked at page 64.

She said no, she hadn't.

I told her to look at page 64 and all would be clear.

She told me to hang on a minute. She set down the receiver, but I could still hear them talking.

"Give me that magazine!"

"Yes dear."

I heard her flipping through the pages, and then the line went dead.

The picture on page 64 showed a muscular young man sporting nothing but a pair of leopard-skin briefs.

Even so, it was six weeks before she let him come out to the bar.

Some people just can't take a joke.

22. Mixed Signals

Scene I

Exterior, Utica, New York, night, a city street
Officers Dewey Duright and Howie Due sit in a parked
police car.

Radio (VO)

This is an APB. Two male suspects wanted for crimes in
Indiana have stolen a vehicle and are reported heading for
Utica. The car is a squaaaawk, squaaawk with New York
plates; license number squaaaawk squeal squaaawkeeeee.

The radio goes silent.

Due

That radio was supposed to have been fixed. 'Course,
for that matter, my wife said the cat was...

Duright

My bookie said the game was...

Due

The repairman said our washer was...

Duright and Due

Y' just can't trust anybody anymore!

Due

That car down at the corner...

Duright and Due

That's them!

Duright

I'm gonna pull them over.

Due turns on siren, they speed up, fade to black

Scene II

Same location: a few minutes later, the same day.
Several police cars, lights flashing surrounding an empty
civilian vehicle, doors ajar. Two men in handcuffs are being
placed in the back seat of a police car.
Due-Duright team stand nearby with the Chief of Police.

The Chief

> Howdy, Due and Duright... and by gum, you certainly
> did do right. Damned if you didn't. Although you
> should have radioed in on the APB.

Due

> Well, Sir, we tried. We only heard the first part, then
> our radio jammed, so we didn't have much to go on,
> and we couldn't contact Dispatch.

The Chief

> Then how did you know this was the stolen car?

Duright

> He gave himself away, sir, sure as a Texan with both
> hands on the wheel.

The Chief

> I don't get you...

Duright

> No self-respecting Texan would steer his truck...

Duright and Due

> ...*with his beer hand!*

The Chief

> Cute, boys, real cute. So what did these *Indianans* do to
> tip you off? Send up smoke signals?

Duright

> You got it, Chief, that's exactly what they did...

Due

> In a manner of speaking...

The Chief
    Get to the point!
Duright
    They signaled, sir, while making a left turn.
Due
    With crazy driving like that...
Duright and Due
    We *knew* they couldn't be from Utica!

Duright, Due and Chief laugh
Cue wacky music
Fade to black

23. Nolo Contendere

Who started the celebration of Christmas? Who added all of the paraphernalia—the gifts, the trees, the cards? Don't tell me, I already know. Besides, I don't want you to confuse me with any facts that run contrary to my preconceived convictions. I don't cotton to having the wool pulled from my eyes.

It had to be the Catholics who invented all this muck. Who else could plan a season so bogged down with guilt? A Jewish mother, you say? Possibly. But I don't know for sure because I never had one of those, having been born the son of a mackerel snapper. No, I'd bet my bingo money it was the Catholics—only the Catholic Church could take mea to such a maxima culpa.

Take presents as an example. You don't take presents—you swap them. To give may not only be better than to receive; in most cases, it's mandatory. Try not giving a gift to your wife this Christmas and watch your jungfrau turn frostier than the K2. But, see, choosing gifts is the worst part of the holiday. We men know this, yet there we are, in Nibsy Ryan's or some other haven at three in the freaking Christmas Eve afternoon saying, "Gotta get the wife sumpin', wadja gitch yers?"

Now, I know what you're thinking: it's our own fault for having procrastinated and prevaricated on proper prognostication as pertains to presents.

But hold still while I parry your glib riposte. We put it off because we *never* know what to get. Yes, we've known for weeks that we have to get her a gift, and all the while we've suffered guilt because we haven't done it yet. And that's where the Catholics come in: in the Mother Church, "guilt" is always a verb. So, you see, we have been doing something about buying gifts; we've been guilting over it.

Then there are those neighbors of mine who rush the season just to tick me off. I mean, the Thanksgiving turkey is still warm in the nice little sepulcher I gave it, and they're out there putting up Christmas decorations! They do that just so I can guilt over it every time I pass their house. About ten days after I get mine up, they take theirs down. No matter how cold it is, they can steel themselves to the task, because it was warm when they put theirs up and they don't have the recollection of freezing their yayas off like I do. So not only do I have guilt for a month before Christmas, but from New Year's Day till the Fourth of July, I have those damn lights nagging me every time I pull in my driveway.

Let's move on to Christmas cards, the hallmark of a whole new approach to guilt. To illustrate my point, here are a few quotes from the Tannenbaum of my life:

"One of these nights, you better plan on staying home so we can make out the Christmas cards."

"For the fifth time, will you please remember to pick up stamps today?"

"Here, put down something nice on this card for your ex-wife's maiden aunt, twice removed."

"Oh, goodness, a card from the Ficklefingers. I think we skipped them this year because they didn't send us one for two years, but then we didn't send them one the year before that, but come to think of it, I don't know how they got on our list anyway because I don't remember ever meeting anyone named Ficklefinger. Are they friends of yours? Friends of your ex-wife? I mean, how did the Ficklefingers get on our list in the first place? Who the hell are the Ficklefingers?"

Next on my Christmas blacklist is the Christmas Visit, which would be more aptly named Christmas Duties. While only Catholics, so far as I know, have to "make their Easter Duty," all of the rest of Christendom are obliged to make their Christmas Duty. Occasionally, we have the joy of seeing the folks we visit squirm because we brought them a little gift and they don't have one for us. The reason they don't have one for us this year is because when they were the ones to visit us last year, we were the ones doing the squirming.

Ah, gift guilt, nothing like it.

Starr takes it upon herself to keep track of who we owe a visit, knowing full well that I would be prone to say things like, "I know they don't like you, and I know you don't like them, and to tell the truth, I don't care for them much either, but they came to see our tree, so we should go over and see theirs. Besides, a son should visit his parents at Christmas time."

Okay, so all of this stuff, we're pretty sure, we can lay on the Catholics. Now, who invented New Years' resolutions? Had to be Calvin, because we know the minute we make them we are destined to fail, it's predetermined. One might even say it was (gasp!) fate.

And, finally, I have the perfect excuse. Yes, it's Christmas Eve again, and yes, I'm buying out the novelties case of my local 7-11, again. But it's not my fault this time: my New Year's resolution last December was shopping early for this Christmas, and New Year resolutions are fated to fail. So, you see, it was fate that put me here. And who am I to argue with what fate gives me?

If only it came gift-wrapped and guilt free.

24. Not a Coffin, a Carload

"**W**hy ask why?" the announcer in the ad asks. I don't like the ad, maybe because I don't understand it. But it sounds like someone's trying to slip one past me. Even in context, it doesn't make sense to me.

But then again, there is an awful lot I don't understand about modern merchandising.

For instance, when you've just wrapped up the purchase of a major new appliance, why does the clerk immediately go into a spiel about the glories of their extended coverage contract? The company automatically guarantees their product for one year, he says, but if you will pony up a paltry sum (equal to about twice the original price of the article), they will unconditionally, positively, absolutely guarantee their product for five additional years.

It's conceivable that you might not see the sense of such a bargain right away. Probably because you're too busy asking yourself, "My God, what have I done? I've just spent how many thousands of dollars for something that, according to what this salesman is now telling me, will last about as long as a sneeze!"

Your hesitation will cause the salesman's mouth to automatically slip into overdrive. "Why, if the main jibber-jobber valve quits working, it's going to cost you eight hundred thirty-eight Washington Irvings to replace it." You mutter something about never having heard of a jibber-jobber valve, and he comes right back with, "Maybe so, but there are six of them in this baby—and that's just on the *left* side."

While you're trying to multiply eight hundred thirty-eight times twelve in your head, but can't due to the sheer magnitude of the cost as compared to the sheer minitude of your bank account, the salesman hasn't stopped talking. (They never do, you know.)

"...against lightning, being lost at sea, complete replacement of all working parts if your child becomes tangled in the works, or even if it's only a teensy weensy fuse, just call us and we'll rush a loaner to your home faster than you can say 'I sure am glad I got the super-duper, hyper-extended, fancy-schmancy, platinum plus, manufacturer's warranty plan.'"

Well, while I was trying to multiply eight-hundred-thirty-eight times twelve in my head, it dawned on me why the salesman does this—he gets a bigger commission for selling the insurance than he does for selling the product.

So I start sussing it out.

I already know that the company makes money on their extended coverage policies or they wouldn't be selling them. But if they're paying this guy such a high commission to sell them, then they must be outrageously overpriced, and I'm a sucker if I go for it. And yet, twelve times eight hundred thirty-eight is a lot of Franklin Delano Reserve notes.

And I know that Murphy's Law, Corollary number 347 (sub-paragraph 2-b) states that if you buy the insurance, you won't need it, but if you don't, you will.

And still, I never know from purchase to purchase what I should do. It's kind of a willy-nilly, fifty-fifty kind of thing. Thus, I will leave it to you, Dear Reader, to decide whether I chose this time to be damned if I did or damned if I didn't.

In any event, after the battle, you go home and relax. You sit down and pop open a beer. But wait! Unless you're an alcoholic, it better not be a Schaefer beer. Because according to their jingle, *"Schaefer is the one beer to have when you're having more than one."*

They obviously don't want moderates as customers.

No, I don't understand modern advertising at all.

Of course, I didn't understand old time advertising, either— take Lucky Strike cigarettes. During World War II, Lucky Strike changed the circles on their packs from green to red, and proclaimed, *"Lucky Strike Green has Gone to War!"* Pretty stupid ad, if you ask me. But that didn't begin to compare to their main slogan, *"Lucky Strike: Not a Cough in a Carload."* Once everyone started to pervert it to "Not a Coffin, a Carload," you'd think

Lucky Strike would have pulled the ad. They never did.
But why ask why?

25. Uncultured Lout

I admit to being uncultured.

I can't hack sculpture, Impressionist paintings don't make a dent, and Mozart is doze-art. Ballet not only looks like it hurts, it's too...too...I don't know; it's tutu something.

And don't get me started on opera! (Too late.) The only welcome sound at the opera comes when the fat lady finally starts to do her thing. Okay, I must admit, I kinda like the way those three burly fellows always try to outdo each other. Sometimes it looks like it might come down to a good old-fashion shoving match. I heard they even inspired a new offensive move in the pro-wrestling world—Tenor's Elbow.

And Nat King Cole was wrong: if Mona Lisa was lovely, I'll eat all of the Playboy centerfolds from 1953 to present—and the wall they're plastered to. I wouldn't let her kiss me with those smirking lips of hers, even if it meant living out the rest of my life as an enchanted frog.

Another thing I find ridiculous is the way our civic leaders install iron sculpture monstrosities in our downtowns—and they use our money to do it. Yet the same stuff is called junk when we showcase it on our own lawn, and by township ordinance must be blocked from view with fences. And they use our money to make us do it.

Okay! I know, beauty is in the eye of the beholder, and one man's meat is another man's poison, and that's fine with me. If you want to spend your hard-earned money to hang a Gains-borough—or a Gainesburger, for all I care—on your wall, it's your money and your wall. But when it's my money, via the tax dollar, that's being seized to support the arts, this Art ceases to be supportive.

If enough people don't voluntarily spend sufficiently to make the arts self-supporting, then the old law of supply and demand should be allowed to take effect. As the buggywhip industry found out, only a horse's ass continues to beat a dead horse. The iceman no longer cometh, having been supersedeth by the icebox. If you're not making something people need, you'd better be making something they want.

Yet mayor after mayor throws buckets of money into downtown areas to "revitalize" them. I understand their problem. They see the great loss in tax revenues caused by businesses moving to the suburbs. They don't see my problem: I'm getting upset watching them futilely chase that lost revenue with more tax dollars. When people wanted downtowns, nobody had to throw millions into them; businesses gladly invested.

But I semi-digress (bet you're not even semi-surprised). If our tax dollars must be spent to support art, why not foster North American art forms? Jazz, Blues, Rock & Roll and Country-Western music; Indian tribal dances, square dancing; oaters, Tarzan movies and musicals...but no, instead we get government funded projects like this:

$7 Million Grant Awarded to Silkscreen Artists
Operating in Service Station Parking Lots:
Half Earmarked for Van Gogh Style Portraits

26. Christmas Trees and Firewood

*T*wo things that I don't like to pay a lot for are firewood and Christmas trees. Shelling out big money for either is like loaning your pet elephant to David Copperfield—everything disappears but the mess.

Firewood is about the most economically negative purchase possible. We pay money for wood, light it on fire, then sit around and watch it disappear. We even invite other people to come and watch us waste our money.

"Come on over, we'll start a fire, have some drinks and play a few games." Before they arrive we clean out the ashes from the last fire, and put in a layer of rolled-up newspapers and kindling. In the hopper next to the fireplace, we stash a careful mix of small-to-large firewood.

When our guests arrive, we can't waste our money fast enough.

And everybody is an expert on how to get it burning faster and better. As soon as someone puts down the poker, the next pyromaniac picks it up and tries to show the previous prodder up. You'd think it was a giant scab. Let it settle down to a small roar and without a doubt someone will say, "Fire's dying out; better throw another log on." We just gotta keep that sucker roaring, nurturing that huge chimney updraft that sucks all of the heat out of the rest of the house, thus increasing our monthly utility bill from a tithe to a quarthe.

It was Adam Smith, the papa of modern economics, who astounded the world with his observation that when you spend more than you take in, you're losing money. How can we better create our own personal deficit than to put our meager wealth up in smoke? Certainly, as an act of conspicuous consumption, Thorstein Veblen—I shite you not, there really was such a man with just such a name who invented the term, "conspicuous consumption"—forgive us, it is the weakest. How many people will actually pass my house and say, "Gee, the Arturoses must be having a very financially successful year; every time I pass their house they have wood smoke coming out of their chimney." Burning dollar bills in Dey Brothers' window would be more effective and a lot more conspicuous. Of course, I'd never stand a chance of burning dollars in Dey Brothers' window, because every time I get near Dey's, Starr grabs whatever money I've got and runs inside to spend it.

Which brings me to shopping. What does? Any mention of Starr and money does. Starr plus my money equals shopping. Well, actually, you really can't call it shopping; the way she does it, it's more of a crusade: The Fifth (Avenue) Crusade.

But wait, I don't really want to get into Starr's shopping yet, because that has to do with Christmas trees, and I'm not done with firewood yet.

How do I not spend money on firewood? I scrounge for it. If I see someone cutting down a big old tree, I axe them if I can have it. If they say no, I split. If they say yes, I split. But first, I pile it into my truck, Big Whitey, and cart it around town for a few weeks. Then when I absolutely need the truck for something else, I unload it. I pick out the smaller pieces when I need firewood, letting the larger pieces season. I avoid splitting any wood before its time. Actually, I avoid splitting any wood before any time; consequently, I have about twenty cords of unsplit wood in my back yard, all in jigunda pieces. And the "smaller" pieces that are left are now so large that one of them will provide an evening's worth of fire—if I can keep it burning.

Okay, now I'm done with firewood, I can devote myself to Christmas trees.

When Starr goes on a quest, she is not looking for a sliver of the True Cross, or any other such minor relic. She wants none other than the Holy Grail, itself. To a true shopper, this means never having to say you're sorry because someone, somewhere, bought whatever it is you bought at a price lower than you paid.

So it is that on one aspect of our life together on this planet, Starr and I agree: we don't want to pay a lot for an adornment that has a life expectancy shorter than Danny DeVito is tall. She does, however, want a big tree. I mean eight feet tall and a zillion feet around. No open spaces in it either. Try getting one of those for five bucks.

And then she found the ad in the Sunday paper: "Christmas Trees $5." Call them up," she said, as she handed me the paper. (There is always one partner in a duo who doesn't like to make calls.)

"I saw your ad. Is that right, five bucks?"

"Yep!"

"Just small ones, right?"

"Nope!"

"How far do I have to walk to see these trees?" You see, I've played this game before. You get to where the ad says, you park your car on the road, and you walk a quarter mile to the farm. From there you are directed via pointed finger to the tree lot "over there." And let me tell you, "over there" looks to be just about past the curvature of the earth. When you have hauled a tree the size that Starr wants from over there to over here, you realize pretty quick that here and there are twains that you don't want to meet again in a hurry.

"Park yer car and yer there."

This guy was getting just too talky for my taste, so I got directions to his farm and rang off.

On the way there, Starr started her fifth degree. "How tall are the trees? Are you sure they're all five dollars? He means five and up, right? Did he actually say that the Austrian pines were five dollars? How many Austrian pines does he have? Did he say his place was six miles west of the thruway, or northwest?"

Why the *#@ does the person who doesn't like to call on the phone always want to know why you weren't more thorough when they stuck you with the job?

No wait, I don't want to let this go. When we have to call

the plumber back to re-fix what he re-fixed yesterday, she always finagles it so that I'm the caller. Yet, according to her standards, I always do it wrong.

What I don't understand is, if I only make local calls, and she is too shy to use the phone, how come our long distance bills are always so high?

When we arrived at the place—and it was exactly six miles east, because I know now that there are no tree farms six miles west—the sign said "$5.00 and up." I spent the first five minutes arguing with a young lot attendant who was insisting that the five dollar price was: (1) for wholesale ("No, no!" I shouted); (2) for balsams ("No, no!" I shouted) and; (3) for the smaller trees. "Bull-gravy!" I shouted. "Your ad mentioned none of those stipulations. When I called, I wasn't told any of those things." I was fighting for my life, man. The day was bad enough without having to spend the rest of it listening to Starr say, "I'd never be one to tell you 'I told you so,' but didn't I?"

We were interrupted by a transplanted New England farmer, who said, "Ayup!" That was it. I was in the right place. That one "Ayup!" proved it. And next he proved that, yes, Virginia, there is a Silvan Clause," because he said, "Ayup! Alla them Scotch, white and Austrian pines is five bucks."

There it was. We were home free. Now it was just a matter of traipsing around in the slosh and the cold for a couple of hours, coming back to one of the first three trees we saw and cutting the sucker down.

The tree we selected was the top eight feet of a very dense thirteen foot tree. The base had a ten foot diameter. Trying to get to the trunk was like crawling into a cave full of burdock and bees. Then you had to hold the branches away with one hand while you sawed (hacked?) away with t'other. About half-way through, the saw started binding and it looked like I'd be there for the next planting, until Mr. Ayup! came by and begrudgingly used his chain saw to finish the cut.

I approached Mr. *Ayup!* and asked what I owed.

"What did I tell you?" he asked.

"Okay, that's five dollars, then," I said.

"Unless you want to give me ten."

"Nope, five," I said, having caught his taciturnity.

Now you probably think that I should have given him the extra five. It was still a helluva deal, and he did help me cut it down after all. But you didn't see the look of euphoric admiration in Starr's eyes when I said, "Nope, five."

It only cost Starr and I two slipped discs each to get it into Big Whitey. Fortunately they all popped back into place when we wrestled the tree into the house.

And once Christmas was over, it made a terrific addition to the woodpile out back.

27. Pure White Trash

I have never had any desire to be a cop. Like the woman on one ski, *Ilene* the other way. My philosophy has always been "T-man, no; T-bill, yes!" But, as Captain Hook told Peter Pan, "Never say never-never, lad."

But now, for the first time, a constabulary job has caught my fancy. (Arrested my interest?). When the new Pure Trash Law goes into effect on July Onest, I want to be Onondaga County's first...*White Trash Trooper*. As the old odor yieldeth to the phew, we must be ready to adapt or die.

I would hire other garbage gleaners to assist me in apprehending those of you who flout the law by not putting your recyclables in those blue bins made of non-recyclable plastic that were distributed throughout the county. My Garbage Gestapo would eventually become more feared than the hordes of Genghis "The Garbageman" Khan, who laid waste to Eurasia way back when. As Czar of Refuse I would have my top spy, Herbert, hoovering around your cellar door waiting for you to mess up—at which time we would trash you good.

I'd need some scientifically trained incisive-decisive-type individuals to develop a secret weapon for me, Der Fuehrer of Filth. I would, therefore, take the coroners off their four-year-old accidental-death-maybe-it's-murder-let's-exhume-once-again-for-old-time's-sake case, and put them on developing a glossy-paper detector. Then you crumb bums who throw out your Sunday paper without going through it page-by-page to make sure you don't miss a throw-away insert that you wish they wouldn't keep inserting in the first place because they keep falling out of the paper and all over the porch when you're out there in your bare feet on freezing winter mornings swearing your head off, will find out just how heavy the long arm of the Dumpster Demigod really is. (Gasp! Pant! Whew! You go on ahead without me. I've gotta catch my breath.)

So, my dirty denizen, it shan't be long before my dog comes around to sniff your can...don't say I didn't warn ya!

(This message is brought you by Big Oil Spill and your Trashional Guard.)

28. Such a Tool!

A number of years ago Starr and I heard a radio ad for the Syracuse University Players. Since she was always looking for something different for us to do as a couple that didn't consist of her watching me win at pool in dingy bars, and since the idea of sitting in an air conditioned theater appealed to me much more than taking a couples-only pottery class, it sounded like just the ticket. So, when Starr suggested we get some (tickets, that is), I said "sure" with nary a "no, please" nor a whining "do I hafta?" She was a bit flummoxed by my uncharacteristically instantaneous acquiescence, but heck, all she hadda do was ask.

On one such theater night, I was running late, so Starr laid out my suit for me. I hurriedly dressed; then she and I hopped in our catering van, and we were off. Ha!

I say "ha" because not only were we were not off, we were most definitely and most decidedly not *on*. When I turned the key, I got nada.

Since this little hiccup had been happening a lot lately, I knew the cause, and I had the cure. The battery had a habit of building up a layer of corrosion on the positive pole, so all I hadda do was undo the connection and steel brush the terminal. Even so, all I could think of was, why me? Why now? If you get there after the play starts, they make you wait out the first act in the lobby before they seat you at intermission. Kinda ruins the whole thing when that happens, doncha know?

Lucky for me, I'd learned to keep the necessary tools in the van, just in case. I disconnected, brushed, and reconnected the battery terminal, then had Starr turn the key. Voilà, it worked! I stuffed the tools in my coat pocket, hopped in, and we were off—this time for real. We literally burned rubber and made it just in time.

After the play, we stopped in at a restaurant for a late supper.

As we were being seated, a customer walked in and handed the bartender a crescent wrench, saying, "Nope, it's too big."

He smirked at her as if to say "that's what they all say" but he held his tongue. Instead, he reached under the bar and handed her a socket wrench. Out she went. A couple minutes later, back she came, shaking her head, "nope, that tool's too big, too."

There was that smirk again. "Sorry, that's all I got."

"That's okay, thanks, anyway."

As she passed by our booth, I said, "excuse me, miss, I couldn't help but overhear. What did you need?"

"Well ideally, a three-eighths inch box wrench, but I can see that isn't gonna..." I held up my finger as if to say "just a sec," then watched her visibly startle as I deliberately reached into my suit coat pocket, producing the very tool she needed.

"Wow!" She exclaimed incredulously, "how did you do that?"

Starr turned to me, laughing, "Oh, Arturo, you are such a tool!"

"Heck," I replied with all the lacon I could muster, "all she hadda do was ask."

29. Spatulum Speculatae

Well, there I was, sitting around, feeling as useless as a saboteur at Nine Mile II*, thinking about what to write this month, but not coming up with anything. Why don't you be serious for a change and tell people some of the things that are in your heart, I thought. So here goes.

One of the closest things to my heart is the rubber spatula. Don't laugh, I'm serious. Think about it: if everybody used a rubber spatula and gleaned the valuable foods we consistently throw away, we could feed all of those starving people in Africa that your mother always harped about. (Mine always harped about the ones in Europe, but things have changed. European mothers now harp about the starving kids in New York City.) The savings would be astronomical. Household budgets would take such a turn for the better, that cats might even start re-appearing on the streets of Solvay.**

To be used, however, they must be handy. So don't put your spatulae in that drawer full of God-knows-what-all doodads. Like the handy jar opener you got from the Kiwanis that pinches your fingers and raises blood blisters, but jars the jar lids ajar not a jot. No, leave your spatulae out, preferably on the kitchen counter. (By the way, what does a counter count?) At least that way they'll be handy to beat the children with when they don't use them on the bowls and jars like you tell them to—which they never do, because they're always looking to do things the easy way—and it's about time you started beating them black and blue instead of just threatening to. And you can always use a spatula when you can't find the fly swatter, if you just keep it near to hand.

Speaking of which, did you know that you can kill flies by clapping your hands just over them? Well, not exactly over them—just a little bit to the front of them. Or is it the back of them? I always forget which. Anyway, flies don't take off at an angle, like airplanes, they fly almost straight up and just a little bit to the front. (Or back—whatever!) Actually, I'm not very good at it. I usually miss hitting my hands together and spill my beer in my lap, or I end up running for my life because I swatted some bruiser next to me. So it's better for my pants and my health to keep a spatula handy.

See? I told you this was serious.

Another subject close to my heart is banking. The other day I sent my wife, Starr, to a neighborhood bank with a check drawn on that bank, made out to "Cash." The teller refused to cash it—not because it wasn't good; it was—simply because it was made out to cash. Starr went to the branch manager, who explained, "Why, just anyone could cash that check."

"I know," said Starr, "I'm just anyone. So please cash it."

"I'm sorry, but I can't do that," she replied.

Starr called me, and I called the manager, who said, "Mr. Arturo, (they're formal like that at banks) it's dangerous for anyone to make out a check to 'cash'. If it's lost, anyone who found it could cash it."

"I know," I said. "But it's your depositor's money, and if he wants to take that risk, it's none of your business."

She still refused to cash the check, so I called my ex-mayor lawyer, Lee (who is, indeed, lawyerly), and asked him if they could do that.

"Definitely not," he said. "A check is a directive to the bank to give a named party—or anyone, if it's made out to 'bearer' or 'cash'—a certain sum of money held in trust for their depositor. They have absolutely no right to refuse."

"Are you sure?" I asked.

"Yes, I know that law inside and out." Well, I trust ex-mayor Lee, and I'm willing to bet that he knows the inside of law pretty darn well. And I'm sure all those on the outside of the law that he's kept from the inside of a prison would say he does, too.

Now, I'm really telling you what is in my heart, so I'm going to tell you something else about banks: "I'm mad as hell and

I'm not going to take it anymore!" I mean, this started out as a pleasant article, but now I'm really getting miffed.

Take the time a bank refused to cash a personal check for $200 for my brother after he had just deposited a bank cashier's check for $4,000. "I'm sorry," the teller said, "but there isn't $200 in that account."

"But you just took my deposit for $4,000."

"I know, but it hasn't cleared yet."

"But it's drawn on a national bank! I'd understand if it was a check from my brother, Art. But it's drawn on a bona fide, FDIC insured bank!"

After getting the same run-around refusal from the head teller and then the bank manager, my brother reached over the counter and retrieved the cashier's check. Crossing out "for deposit only," he re-signed the check, which the teller cashed for him. He put $200 of it in his pocket and, in a second transaction, deposited the rest into his account.

The obvious solution is for every bank to have rubber spatulas on their counters, so that we could slap those tellers black and blue when they need it.

*Nine Mile II was at the time suffering from missed deadlines.

**There has been a persistent urban legend that they eat cats in Solvay. The origin of this legend is unbeknownst to me—or to anyone beknownst to me.

***You knew I was only kidding about beating your children with a spatula, didn't you? You should never do that—it leaves a mark. Use a rolled up newspaper, instead. Or, better yet, hit 'em over the head with a bank manager. That'll teach 'em both.

30. Starr Power

Starr wanted more kitchen cupboards.

She had been dropping hints for years; hints about as subtle as Mr. T is demure. About fourteen months ago she started dragging me around home improvement stores, "just to look." Being dragged is, of course, the only way a wife gets a husband out shopping for anything except maybe a new shotgun, but I think your chances of seeing that are about as good as seeing Mr. T in a pink tutu.

When I saw the prices they were asking for the cupboards, I said, "When I get time, I'll make you some—can't be all that hard." Actually, I had no such intention; I was just using a ploy that all husbands are forced to use when our wives are on our backs. It's called buying time, and it costs a hell of a lot less than coughing up money right now. "Let me think about it," is interpreted by all wives as a definite yes, but it at least sets completion time someplace in never neverland.

Now, I can hear you married male readers snickering—you've been there, haven't you? But unless you've got more guts than the guts I've got, you dast not come out with a flat "No!" Well, not unless you want a wife as warm as an Eskimo's grave in the wintertime, you dasn't.

Now the political maneuvering begins. She tries to box you in while you stall for time. Politics is not my forte. In the last five presidential elections, I voted for the winner every time, and you saw what that got us. And I'm up against one of the greatest tacticians of all time. She's as wily as Rommel, as merciless as Genghis Khan, and as relentless as Hannibal. Give her any guff and she'll pull a Patton on you.

One of her more brilliant tactical maneuvers went like this:

Last Christmas she bought me a radial arm saw; for Father's Day, a circular saw; for my birthday, a jig saw and table. Along about September she started reporting to me every time our granddaughter, Amina, put another penny in her piggy bank. "Poor kid," Starr would sigh, "saving every cent she's got for that dollhouse. She's really got her heart set on it, but I just don't think it's gonna happen. Too expensive."

Then she offhandedly mentioned, "I grabbed the wood from that old picnic table you trashed, and stuck it in the cellar, you never know when it will come in handy."

Cue the cute anecdotes. "Amina was over today. You know those old wooden orange crates in the cellar? She started pretending they were a dollhouse, and she was telling her dolls all about how Grandpa had built the dollhouse just for them, and how it was just like Grandpa and Grandma's house. I wish you could have seen her, she was so cute."

Do you see the subtle plot forming? Sure, Starr wants our granddaughter to have a dollhouse. That's obvious—but there's more to it than that. Her modus operandus up until now has always included healthy doses of motives ulterius, plannus sinisteria—and games, my dear Watson, that are more than afoot; they're at least a country mile.

But, alas, the doting grandfather is trapped—hoisted by his own wife's petard. There's nothing I can do but build the dollhouse. How can I refuse, and still face the sweet face of my darling grandchild? I have been outmaneuvered by political ployage in the superpluperfect and Starr's hidden agenda comes unhidden unbidden. To wit:

One: in order to build the dollhouse, she reasoned, I must uncrate all those tools she had so thoughtfully stockpiled in the guise of gifts, and actually learn how to use them. Two: building the dollhouse would give me the experience needed to build those damn cabinets. And, three: I was going to build those damn cabinets!

In truth, I have only myself to blame—I didn't know how great a BS artist I was. Starr really believed me when I said I could build such things! I never told her that there are only two things in the world that leave me mystified, and they are the Federal Reserve System and power tools.

Amina did, however, get her dollhouse (of sorts) and I did learn a few things about power tools in the process. For instance:

When they named the Jig Saw, they left out its middle name, Jag.

Never hold your hand in front of a staple gun to see if it's loaded.

The circular saw is so named because any cut made with it, if extended far enough, will come back in a circle. Or so it is my experience. All of my attempted straight cuts look like the path taken by the bow-legged man whose cross-eyed wife told him to go straight home.

The number on the back of sandpaper sheets does not mean how many are in the pack. Pick too low a number (or is it too high?) and you can turn out some pretty neat looking shingles.

A radial arm saw has two 45-degree settings. Ha! On the left side, it actually cuts at 44.8 degrees and on the right, at 45.2 degrees. Extended out to two feet, that silly little less-than-one-percent difference results in one wall (of a dollhouse, say) being two inches higher than the other. (I think it kind of gives it character.)

A miter box might; then again, it might not. And why the hell do they call it a box, anyway, when it only has three sides?

The router is a definite improvement over the stone chisel. I find the crazy cuts they make to be identical, but the router makes them much faster.

Fortunately, my brother is a woodworking marvel. He taught me the art of wood putty compensation. (I'm still looking for a place that sells it in five gallon buckets.) I guess I didn't do too badly though; my granddaughter is playing with her dollhouse now and loves it. Of course, we can't forget that this is the same easy-to-please child who found architectural grandeur in two orange crates.

Excuse me—a lumber truck has arrived in my driveway

and Starr is calling me down to the kitchen. Golly-gee-willickers, I wonder what she could have ordered? I hope it's the demure Mr. T in a tutu. I could definitely use the help.

31. That's My Conspiracy Theory...

...and they're sticking it to me. Yes, my friends, there is a conspiracy underfoot (they seldom happen overhead, you notice, though they do elicit a gut-level response). Its main objective is the keeping of one particular person an outcast, an outsider.

I am here to tell you I am that outcast. I am that outsider. My name is Arthur J. Belge and this is my story.

I first noticed it during my eighth summer on this planet, the summer that UFOs were featured in the news.

I had just come back from a week at a friend's camp where he and his brother had introduced me to the fine arts of whittling, fishing and the, um, spilling of seed on infertile ground, to find everyone talking about UFOs. Since my attempts to, um, seed the earth had been unsuccessful (yes, too young to raise the sickle), it was the second time in a fortnight that everybody was talking about a strange phenomenon I knew nothing about. I felt like I was from another planet! And everyone I talked to knew someone who had talked to a person whose friend had actually seen a UFO. Somehow, I had been left out; the world was passing me by. I was overpowered by the belief that everybody was having amazing experiences—everyone, except for me.

As I grew, so did the conspiracy. Just to keep me alienated, whenever I did something exceptional, people would make up rules to negate my achievement. Ridiculous rules, such as:

—Each team has its own basket.
—Unless you have the baseball, they are not "out" when you knock them down.
—On a quarterback sneak, the ball must remain outside the quarterback's jersey.

If you doubt that this proves conspiracy, let me add one fact—as soon as someone made one of these previously unstated rules up, everyone swore to it! And the girls were in on it, too!

And the conspiracy continues. When I go into a supermarket I have the feeling everybody knows the rules but me. If I get into the 8-items-or-fewer line, I get dirty looks from other customers. Three cans of soup for a dollar—is that one item or three? How about a bunch of bananas selling for three pounds for a dollar? Do I have one, three or ten items? Is a case of beer one case, four six packs, or twenty-four bottles? I don't even think about buying a bunch of grapes if I'm in a hurry.

I stopped in a market in North Syracuse that had express lines marked *Fifteen Items*. What the hell does that mean? It just boggles the mind. For that matter, what is a boggle? A small swamp? An Irish trumpet?

This past Sunday I went out to Oneida Lake to do a little fishing. When I got three-quarters of the way down the road to the boat ramp, I found an hour-long line of vehicles waiting to use the launch. Can you believe it? They had actually engineered a bass-fishing tournament just to keep me off the lake!

Undaunted, I waited my turn, watching people carrying baskets of bass to the weigh station. Finally, I launched. I fished for hours. I never got a bite. I used live bait, dead bait, crank bait and yank bait (not the same as on the first page of this essay, you better betcha not.) How did all of those people catch all of those fish? Conspiracy, that's how! They all knew something I didn't know and they made damn sure I never learnt it.

Somewhere there is a secret club where all those guys share four things: the right time, the right place, the right bait and a solemn vow not to let Art know any of the first three, upon pain of death.

You know, I remember back in the thirties asking my mother where babies came from. She gave me a song and dance about saving pennies to buy them from a hospital.

My lord! Even my mother is part of it! I'm doomed!

32. The Half Gospel According to St. Tepid

A s I passed a church the other day, I noticed their sign, *Full Gospel*.

But before we get to that, a few annunciations. First, it would be a fair assumption on your part that I am a devout believer in passing churches. I give them wide berth; they attract too much of the unsavory element, don't you know. Adulterers, liars, thieves—sinners of every sort. Second, they always cost money, and all you ever get for that money are re-runs. Third, now that the Mass is no longer in its mother tongue, the mystique is gone and it's even more boring. And fourth, when I committed matrimony with my second wife I was automatically excommunicated from the Catholic Church. So I hold about as much truck with them as they hold with me.

Now, I don't mean to sound truculent or extremely unctuous, but I do have a confession. When I found out that the mass of us dissenfrankencensed didn't have to suffer the penance of getting up on Sunday mornings anymore, I felt that my hanging had been done with velvet ropes. Years later, when the Church decided that we gay divorcées could be allowed back into the fold, I simply rolled over and went back to sleep.

I thought about the full gospel being offered in that church, and by gosh, do you know, I couldn't for the life of me remember ever seeing a half gospel in church. Have you? Logically, they must exist or we wouldn't need full gospels.

What is the gospel like, I began to wonder, that these half-godspellers preach? Would Saint Stephen be their patron saint—he, who while being burned at the stake, requested to be turned over because he was done on one side? By what bench- (pew?) marks would we recognize the half-gospel?

Easter announcement: Hallelujah! Christ is recovering nicely after a run-in with a band of roamin' soldiers and a mild case of cruci-fiction.

...and the Samaritan came upon a fork in the road...

We have a report that the walls of Jericho may have suffered damage.

St. Paul preaches that to be a good Christian, one must obey the five commandments and make love unto thy neighbor as thou wouldst unto thyself.

The debate over which is the half sin of the Three-and-a-Half Deadly Sins has fractionalized the Church.

The clergy would attend semi-seminaries in charcoal-gray suits with unstarched collars. Nuns would not have habits—maybe just a few peccadilloes.

Money would be raised through half-baked sales, Someday collections, and an annual Peter's ha' penny collection and fund-raising walk.

But I think the most alluring attribute of the Church of the Half-Gospel would have to be the services themselves. No more knee-breaking sit-stand-kneel, sit-stand-kneel while the preacher drones on and on. Instead, it will be a few hymns (*A-Hazy Grace*), a quick call-and-response sermon ("Did you sin?" "Yes, we did!" "Well, cut it out!"), and an offering of the Host (white, wheat or sourdough) with a grape-juice chaser.

After giving this all the thought it deserves (one-Mississippi, two-Mississippi), I've come to a conclusion. Whether the wine goblet is half full or half empty, or the sermon is on the mount or on a mound, we sinners can rest easy in our God-given right to roll over and go back to sleep.

And to that, I say, "Amen!"

33. The Sting of Il Padrino

The Mark

Ya gotta watch out fer Mario. He's sly—just how sly yer gonna find out in a minit—always workin' a angle. I've knowed him for years and we been trew jinx so high and capers so low dat ya got a development where ya eader hate each udder or yer buddies. We're real good buddies, so he's usual pretty straight wid me. It comes as not unlikely den, when he axes me to be godfodder to his new son, Rocky.

The Set-up

"But, Mario," sez I. "I been excommunerated, and a godfodder ain't spose to be no trown away Cathlic. Like, if I go inta a church even St. Christophah would laugh and trow his medals at me." Mario comes back wid a argament, da logistics of which can't be refused: "The old lady wants it inna church; yer my buddy an I want you." He's played his ace and I ain't got no trump. "Okay! Fer you I'll do it."

The Hook

"Just one ting," Mario sez. "Ya gotta get a paper from yer paster dat sez yer a good Cat'lic."

I love da guy, but see what I mean about bein' sly? He waits till I say yes, den he slips a hook like dat in.

The Hustle

So, I stops by da choich and says, "Hiya, Fodder! I phoned ya up about dat paper I need ya to sign." "Yes" sez da great black bear. "But since your call, I checked our records and you aren't receiving tithing envelopes, so how do I know that you're an upstanding church member?"

Now I'm in deep water...and it ain't Holy. I gotta tink fast. It's obvious dat a good Cathlic pays his dues and den he can sin if he wants to. But me, all I been doin is dueless sinnin. So I sez, "Well, gee, Fodder, mebbe I fergot to sign up, but ya wouldn' want me to go to some udder parish and lie and tell em I was goin' dare, woodja?" He don't like it, but he sez "Okay," and I had my paper dat sez I stand good.

The Sting

A coupla months later I get a call at work from da ol' ball and chain. "What's goin on?" she sez. "Four ladies from the Alter & Rozary Saciety kept me on the stoop for an hour, naggin' me I should join. And what's more, some kids delivered church envelopes a week ago, and yesterday the mailman delivered the Cathlic Sun!"

"You member Rocky's christnin' a couple weeks ago? I hadda buy a few subscriptions so da priest would sign da paper dat sez I could be Rocky's godfodder. An ya know what?" says I. "I thot I was connin da fodder, but I'm not so shur now. Dat baby christenin' was weeks ago and ain't nobody axed me fer dat paper yet."

34. To Catch a Neighborhood Thief

Do you remember your first bike? Of course you do! It was a step, a very large step in your quest for freedom. Any store, friend's house, or center of entertainment was now within your reach. It was like you had wings. You probably even pretended that you did. I know I did! (Pretend, that is, not have wings.)

One of my six girls had just gotten her first bike a week or so before. She listened (attentively, I thought) to my sermon on the mounting which included such dicta as "Mount and dismount so that you are on the curbside of the bike, do not ride double, train your eyes and ears so that you know what is going on around you, et cetera."

All she forgot was the "lock the door" part of "Put your bike in the garage and lock the door." She didn't even shut it.

The bike, as you might have guessed, was stolen.

I asked the kids of the neighborhood if they had seen anyone who was riding a bike they had never seen them on before. "Yes," a couple of them said, "Johnny Weisenheimer has one," and they described my daughter's bike. I went to the Weisenheimer's house and told his mother what I had learned. She said she would ask her son about it when he came home from school, but she didn't believe that he would make a habit of doing such a thing. A lot of things seem unbelievable. I didn't really believe he made going to school a habit either.

I wondered what glass bubble she was living in, since the first stop the police made when something went missing in our area was her house.

Sure enough, she reported to me the next day that her son denied knowing anything about a stolen bike. What about the one he was seen riding?" I asked.

"He told me he borrowed it from his friend, Manny Criminalis, and my son never lies."

Wow! I thought, I have seven children and they are all good kids, but some of them are exquisite liars.

My synapses started firing like a Gatling gun.

"Lady," I said, "the police department has detailed a detective to our residential area because there are so many minor crimes. The detective told me that if he could stop your son and his friends he wouldn't be needed here and he could be reassigned to an area in the Tenderloin district. Friends of your son told me that not only was your son a liar, he was the one who headed the robbery of your own little business. Do you hear me lady? Your own sanctified son of a_____ and his buddies broke in and stole your opening change bank from your cash register!

"The police said they couldn't prove it! And he told me he didn't do it," she screamed.

I sat down on the curb, repeating, "He who loses his temper first, loses the argument. He who loses..."

After an hour or two, I picked myself up and went home to my daughter. It broke my heart to tell her that her bike had probably been sold on the North Side black market by now and I wouldn't be able to finance a replacement. It was a harsh lesson, but the rememberies section of her medulla oblongata must have been greatly improved by giving her the stick instead of a carrot, because she turned out to be a very responsible adult.

Then again, maybe it wasn't so much losing the bike that changed her for the better. It might have been seeing little Johnny Weisenheimer being hauled off to Juvenile Hall a few months later that did the trick.

I know it made *me* feel better.

35. Uncle Sam Wants...Moi?

*D*uring the second war after The War to End All Wars, Uncle Sam cocked his finger at me, and I'm sorry, but I thought that was very rude. Not only was he pointing, which I'm sure his mother, Betsy Ross, told him was socially taboo, but he definitely wasn't inducing me into induction with that scowl on his face. Let him send all of the letters he wanted, with the word *"GREETINGS"* in the tallest and boldest print possible; still I wanted no part of what he was selling, which was the regimentation and untimely demise of one Arthur J. Belge. These were two things which I have always found personally distasteful and morally objectionable. Untimely meant anytime within the next century as far as I was concerned, and I was most definitely concerned; and getting regimentated sounded like it hurt.

Moreover, I was an almost-second-time father and a college almost-graduate needing just two one-semester courses to complete my degree. I wrote a letter explaining this to the Draft Board, and that my wife was carrying our second child. While neither of these qualified me for exemption, I explained I would appreciate a six month stay, after which I would gladly (ha!) report as directed. They were very sympathetic. They sent me a letter telling me to report for my physical and gave me a date for a hearing to plead my case.

The hearing date was the day before my departure date. God, I hoped my plea was accepted.

Up until that time, the only army I had ever been in was the Boy Scouts, and that only lasted two weeks. Some of the guys had seduced me into joining with their talk about learning neat stuff like tying a zillion different knots, earning merit badges and going on camping trips. But nobody, as in N-O-B-O-D-Y, mentioned the military aspect of the organization. There I was, at my first meeting, waiting for all this good shit to start, when the Scout

Obermeister started calling out, "Tenderfoot Burns, FRONT AND CENTER! Tenderfoot Graham, FRONT AND CENTER!" And, one by one, I'm watching my heroes—guys who made nuns pray each night for martyrdom or a transfer; and it really didn't matter which, as long as it was before school the next morning—perform precise, heel-clicking corner-turns to the tune of some neo-Nazi fascist martinet.

Inside, I'm screaming, "Guys, this ain't where it's at! We have the Black Bears five days a week, marching us in and out of the school building to a scratchy rendition of *Stars and Stripes Forever*. With their "no talking and sit up straight with both hands folded together on the desk" and "wipe that smile off your face, Master Belge." And their favorite, "Very well, we will all just sit here after school until the guilty party owns up."

The nuns knew there was good reason for all of these rules, especially the "both hands on the desk" rule, because if the boy's hands were out of sight, they might be...be...well, it's a rule— that's why!

The Boy Scouts looked like more of the same. After that first meeting I asked the guys, "What do we need this for?"

The boys didn't listen to me way back then, and I was sure Uncle Sam wasn't going to listen to my irrationalizations now. So I reported for my physical, as-ordered-SIR!

Those of you who have never been called for a military physical might as well stop reading, because you'll never believe I didn't make the rest of this up. Those that have been in the service will shake their heads and say, "Been there, seen that."

After making us fill out tons of paperwork and take a written test, they had us strip and line up for the eye exam. "Why didn't they have us strip before the written stuff, then they could freeze our butts off longer?" The guy behind me muttered. He realized his error when he saw a military-type-person write his comment down. Perhaps he thought it was a good idea that he could pretend was his own at the next staff meeting, but "Whispers" and I strongly suspected that unless you're a five-star, it is not healthy to have your words written down.

"BROWN, JOSEPH!" the sergeant stentored. A fellow stripling, two bodies up from me halfheartedly waved a hand.

Those of us nearby could hear Sergeant Stentor grilling Brown. "Wha'd'ya mean by this word on your questionnaire?"

"Just what it says."

That question and answer, variously phrased, cleared the net several times before Brown, Joseph in exasperation lobbed the ball out of bounds, saying, "Gay means gay."

"Well, maybe that means you're happy, and maybe it means somethin' else, but I'll let it go for the moment." (In Brown's and Stentor's defense, we are talking 1950s mores: a time when closets were built with heavier hardware. People did not come right out and say the word "homosexual.")

It was then that I noticed that the guy behind me, an old high school pal, was mumbling a litany. "Praying for a heart murmur?" I asked.

"No," said he. "I can't see without my glasses, so I'm memorizing the eye chart as each guy says it. That way I can pass the test when it's my turn."

I didn't have the heart to tell him that first prize was a ride through downtown Seoul on a claymore.

But this guy wanted to be drafted, against his mother's wishes. I met him again years later, and learned he'd been successful...to a point. He did pass the physical and went through basic training like he was riding a water park sledge. But when they found out he had a year of college, they kept him in the States to train other recruits. After several months he got tired of this, so he went to the aide and asked to see the base commander and was told, "Not on your life!" Undaunted, he walked into the head honcho's office anyway and blurted out, "I'm here to fight, not babysit! Please send me where the action is."

"I could have you court-martialed and sent to Leavenworth for insubordination, but we need fighters. I admire your courage. Pack up, you leave at dawn." He did, and they shipped him off.

It so happened that one in three hundred soldiers were sent to Germany; the other two hundred ninety-nine went to Korea where the action was. So who did they send to Germany? The one guy who wanted to fight! He ended up playing haus with some frau until he was discharged at the end of the krieg. Go figure!

"ALRIGHT BROWN! What's with this note from your minister that says you're a pacifist? We're going to give you a gun so you can either shoot the enemy or shoot yourself in the foot. Or we could use you as fodder and deliver you by cannon. And what's with this note from your mother's chi-row-practicer, saying that he thinks you might have weak kidneys and ain't got no control?"

Brown (sotto voce), "I wet the bed."

"The army don't recanize chi-ro-practicers, so for all chi-ro-practical intents and purposes, haw-haw, this doctor an' his note don't exist. If you got weak kidneys it's probably cuz-a lacka exercise cuz you choke your chicken with a limp wrist." Sarge thought this so funny that he roared—uproariously, of course—tears streaming, as he staggered down the hall. Evidently, he needed to share this gem of latrinal humor before it flushed itself from his tiny working memory.

I was still several men down the line when I overheard one doctor saying to another, "Nah, those feet are okay—I've passed worse than that. They'll be a stabilizing influence in high winds." Maybe so, but as I glanced at the soles of interest, I saw feet so large and so flat, it looked like somebody let all the air out of the dude's ankles.

My attention was next attracted to a hubbub on my left as one of the doctors called the first names of his colleagues and pointed to the recruit in front of him. Having been told to bend over'n spread his cheeks, the poor rube had responded with an innocence that would make his mother proud. Facing the doctor, he bent at the waist, crooked his fingers in the sides of his mouth, spread his cheeks, waggled his tongue, and said "ahhh."

Then it was Brown's turn again. "A sixth grader can pass the written test you took AND FAILED today. You graduated from high school. You're signing on somewhere today Brown, Fort Dix or Fort Leavenworth. Choose!"

Poor Brown...the fellow had pulled out all of the stops, but it was obvious his tactics were not going to work.

Whispers put on his best smile as he approached Sergeant Stentor. "Pardon me Sarge, but did you notice on my questionnaire, where I listed my occupation as a minister in the Walk-on-Your-Heels-and-Save-Your-Souls Faith? You see, we believe..."

"Can it!" Stentor cut in. "I ain't gonna take no more shit from nobody." But we noticed just a little smirk sneak into the corner of his mouth. And that was the key that freed us all as we laughed our asses off. I wasn't sure, however, that the Army had a fully developed sense of humor, so I again refrained from pointing out to Sarge his penchant for double negatives.

The next day, along with about twenty others, I showed up at the Draft Board at 1:00 pm. I waited as each one of us was called in, in no apparent order. Finally, I sat there alone. I was last. Did that mean something? If so, what? Did the other twenty have more serious impediments to service, so their cases took precedence? Were their deferments being granted? There had been a paucity of smiles on their faces, as one by one they returned from their hearings.

Finally it was my turn. They let me state my case and told me to wait in the outer office. As the door was closing behind me, I heard the only woman on the panel say, "He does not qualify. Why should we..."

As I sweated it out, awaiting the verdict, I tried to console myself. She didn't really mean that—she was probably playing Devil's Advocate like they do in Rome when the Church is looking into a possible canonization candidate. Or she *is* the devil and she's going to sway the panel and it's "Bye-bye, Artie!"

They called me back in.

"We are going to grant your request for a deferment. But I'm sure you know what that means."

"No, ma'am." I thought it meant I wouldn't be drafted right away, but the question threw me. Did it mean I'd have to serve longer after a deferment than I would without it? Or that I'd be at the bottom of the military totem pole, given even more hopeless, pointless assignments than most recruits? "Private Belge! Take this flag and run across enemy lines, we need to see what kind of armament they've got!"

But no, it really was good news. "Didn't you see the evening paper? President Eisenhower has signed a bill exempting fathers from the draft. So by the time your deferment expires, you will be exempt."

Well, that cast a new light on fatherhood! I went right home and started making more babies. Eventually, my wife and I had seven, keeping me safe at home all the way through that, um, police action, and the one after that, and the one after that, and all I have to say is...God Bless America!

36. Walk on Your Heels and Save Your Souls

A good businessman looks for a void and fills it. Being a good businessman with a successful pizza shop to prove it, I sense a current vacuum in the religion-for-bucks field. I intend to step in and build a new organization that will utilize modern technology, avail itself of the leadership talent not currently being fully employed, and update the outdated concepts of old-time religion.

The first thing I'm going to do is lighten things up a bit. (Fulton Sheen recognized the need for this, when he said that the man who said that the pun was the lowest form of humor was obviously a man who couldn't think of one.) The elders of religion had no sense of humor: too full of the straight and narrow-mindedness of thou-shalt-nots, bleating beatitudes, and valley-of-the-shadow-of-death frames of mind. I mean, who enjoys being around someone who's always breaking stone tablets and beating up on money changers? And consider poor Lot's wife's lot, or the raw deal the Sodomites and Gomorrans got just for partying.

Having learned respect for those organizations that have shown great ability at bringing in the bucks, I will adopt their techniques. The Catholics with their multiple collections will have nothing on me. Ten minutes after requesting radio listeners send in their donations, I will request that they send in another for twice the amount. I will appoint the Pope as administrator of our investments. A good money manager is worth his tithe in gold, if he can fill our vaults as full of riches as the Vatican catacombs.

I will make appointments of other capable people I feel are currently being under-utilized. Jim Baaker will be in charge of selling dispensations and indulgences—especially self-indulgences. When we move into the marketplace, I'm sure the Pope will agree that Tammy should be in charge of such acquisitions as Aunt Jemima's Pancakes, National Cement and Revlon Cosmetics, whose value she will increase by mixing them all together under a conglomeration, sorry, I mean conglomerate, called Aunt Revelation's Cosmetic Cement.

Having put this enterprise on a firm foundation, she will package cosmetics kits that our mendicants will sell door-to-door. They will be all-purpose kits containing not only rouge, mascara and the like, but the necessary applicators: trowels, stucco sprayers, chisels, etc.

Edwin Meese III will be in charge of the morals police and insider trading.

Clerical positions will be filled by Jessica Hahn from the "Positions Wanted" section of the *Las Vegas Post*. Our churches will be open-air churches—well, actually, they'll be a national string of golf courses. That way we start with a membership of half of the population, who can honestly say, "Church!" when asked where they were Sunday morning. In the clubhouse, candle racks will be replaced by slot machines, and the confessionals will be marked "Truth and Consequences" on the left, and "Possible Screenplays" on the right.

Sunday morning service will include devil-wrestling bouts with your favorite commentator and an ex-wrestler, Offal Roberts. Our theme park will feature a stone-throwing contest and such attractions as The Holy Roller Roller Coaster, The Holy Ghost's Haunted House, The Virgin Mary-Go-Round (catch the brass halo for a free ride), and the Hammer of the Righteous Test of Faith.

Jerry Falwell will change his last name to Arise-well and each week will perform the grand finale: raising somebody really worthwhile from the dead (say, James Dean or Jayne Mansfield). After several months, when we have everyone's attention, he will astound the nation by breathing life into Kaiser Motors—or maybe even Sly Stallone's acting.

As you can see, I am set to make a mint in my new religio-business. But if not...there's always pizza.

37. What a Bummer Winter Is, I Long to Be Where Flowers Riz

In our complex world we tend to look down on simple adages, labeling them as trite, and thereby poo-pooing the succinct truths they convey. There are those of us, however, who still find wisdom in the maxims of Yore (a country located between ancient Rome and Greece, populated by Franklin, Lincoln, Shakespeare and the patriarchs of the Bible, who are the only accepted sources for maxims), and live by the ideas espoused in such tenets as the New England ethic: dump it, recycle it, or give it to the Salvation Army.

Can one deny the basal truth of the following?

"God loves you." (Bzzz...swat.) "Go to God, little fly." Mahatma Gandhi

"In heaven there is no beer—to hell with that." Billy Carter

And my two favorites now that winter has set in:

"Into each life a little rain must fall, but don't bitch, at least you don't have to shovel rain."

"The Lord giveth snow and we'll just wait for the Lord to taketh the snow away."

The latter statement shows how much I've changed over the years. I used to think—you're not going to believe this—but I used to think that people who didn't shovel their walks were uncivic jerks. Not so. It turns out I was the anti-sociable one. Apparently, everyone but me had a meeting and decided that we should not fly in the face of Mother Nature. We should simply wait for the snow to melt away in its own time.

So now I leave the sidewalk alone like everyone else, and drive everywhere I go, even if it's just down the block. Or else I stay indoors. Problem solved.

This new conventional wisdom also tells us that winter's

greatest danger is the shock of going from the warmth of the indoors to the coldth of the outdoors, so we should do as little of that as possible.

To illustrate this point, I would like to retell a story of my dad's. He swore this story was true, but he was known to—well, never mind, he was my dad, after all.

It seems he went to visit a friend in the hospital. When my father arrived, another visitor, an old farmer, was jumping up and down screaming, "They kilt my brother! They kilt him! I brung him in yesterday and today he's dead. Damn fool nurses, first thing they do is give him a bath—in the middle of winter! Ain't no way to treat a well person, let alone a sick one!"

What I'm trying to say is, there are times when retention of sanity demands a change in lifestyle: I used to go outside in the winter, now I don't. But if we're going to do it, I say, let's really do it. If we're going to make changes, we should go all the way. I'm not talking about just switching from whiskey to gin. I'm talking about some serious adaptations.

Outdoor sports such as golf and football must give way to indoor skiing. Skiers must have gloves by Gucci, goggles by RayBan, poles by Jaruzelski, coats by Hart, Schaffner and Gorbachev (Marx is currently out of vogue, of course), under- wear by K-Mart, and a sympathy leg cast by Velcro. Skis are not required or advised.

Basketball must give way to pastimes like poker and lying naked in front of the fireplace.

Which reminds me of a story told to me by a hairdresser who worked in a salon next to the old Arturo's—and I swear she swore it was true. A customer of hers was always bragging about the legion of lovers in her life, which our hairdresser doubted. Having no evidence to the contrary, and since the lady was, after all, a customer, my neighbor stoically listened each time to her supposed latest high jinks. And then one day, the customer just went too far: she claimed to have gone out with Jack Smith. Not only did she go out with him, she said, but they'd ended up spending the night lying in front of his fireplace, naked. Unbeknownst to the customer, the hairdresser herself was dating Jack Smith, and she knew that Jack would never date this frump. Enough was enough!

"I've been in Jack's apartment," the hairdresser exclaimed, "and Jack doesn't have a fireplace!" With hardly a heartbeat's hesitation, the customer condescended, "Every man has a fireplace, my dear; you just have to know how to stoke it."

See? Those old sayings have some truth in 'em, after all.

38. What a Gas, Man!

I received many comments about last month's column; and believe it or not, they weren't all "That was stupid, Art!" or "You forgot the punch line!" Surprise! I wrote something everybody liked for a change (except maybe Mom, who after reading it, gave me one of her disgusted, you've-soiled-your-pants-again looks). So I decided to continue with the same topic this month.

For those of you who just tuned in (and didn't tune out somewhere in the opening paragraph), last month I rambled on about the goings-on at the old corner gas station. Join me while I continue to digress, always remembering that digression is the bitter part of detour.

Primo and Segundo, the two brothers who ran the garage in question, had a bipartite philosophy with two parts:

Part I: Avoid getting involved in tricky repairs. They take too much time, thus costing more than you can charge for them—while they force you to ignore the rest of your customers.

Part II: Never screw around with gas tanks, they will screw back.

I liked their philosophy. It made excellent business sense, and I am the best of businessman, after all. (Is that the same as being the best of businessmen, bar none? I hope not, I like bars.)

The brothers had a young man working for them, we'll call him George. To this day George and I are good buddies. We both like to fish, and he doesn't drink—which works out great for me, after all, someone has to drive us to, and especially from, the lake. And neither of us likes to admit when we're wrong, and we're both as stubborn as newborn ketchup.

George also had a two-part philosophy of the bipartite persuasion:

Part I: The best thing about being a mechanic is seeing what makes things tick. For George, it was a great trick to take a tick that ought to tock, and by tinkering or taking a new tack, get that tock back on track, tick-nically speaking.

Part II: You can repair a gas tank, if you fill it with water and are very, very careful.

I liked his philosophy, too—I'm a LeMoyne College graduate, and one thing the Jesuits like in their students is a liking of philosophy. I especially liked George's philosophy in combination with the brothers' philosophy, because it meant that no matter what went wrong with your car, one of the three of them would be able and willing to fix it. Their bipolar bipartite predilections formed a symbiotic bipartisanship, by gum.

For example, I remember the pickle I was in that had me gherkin my hair out when the rod connecting my truck's gas pedal to the carburetor broke. My truck was about as utile as those cut-out hand-holes they put in flimsy cardboard boxes. Segundo Brother tried to order me a rod, but found that it would take a minimum of three weeks to arrive. What to do? A little thinking outside the gearbox was required. So it was George to the rescue: he fashioned a replacement rod from a length of steel.

One day, a gas station across the street from the brothers' station became available, and George took it over. George and the brothers remained friends even though they were now in competition. They both adhered to their private dichotomous philosophies and felt no need to denigrate each other to customers.

Primo Brother suspected that George occasionally repaired gas tanks, but knowing George's stubbornness didn't make a to-do about it. George, knowing Primo's feelings, and also knowing how Primo would lecture him about it, never admitted it.

One day Primo heard a BOOM and came running out of his office to see smoke pouring out of the window seams and from underneath the closed overhead doors of George's station. Primo ran across the street as George came stumbling out of his garage. His hair was singed, his eyebrows were gone, and he was covered in soot.

"Are you hurt?" Primo asked, grabbing George's shoulders

to steady him.

"I'm fine. Why do you ask?"

"The explosion! The big explosion! The whole neighborhood shook!"

"Oh, that," George said. "Just a bit of a carburetor backfire, there."

Primo went back to his garage, muttering, "Carburetor, my ass!"

George went back to his garage, grumbling, "Everybody has to make such a big deal over nothing."

And me? I figured it would take at least three weeks for my new gas tank to arrive...

39. Philly's Phinest

Alicia was a pretty blonde with a winsome way that attracted men. You just wanted to cuddle her and take her home and tell your dad, "Look what I found. Can I keep her please, please?" And your dad would say "Absolutely, Son. You've done well." She seemed to bring out that protectiveness that some men have toward such women—and, boy, did she know how to use it!

She told of the occasion—a few years before we met her—of dating a young man who was a student in Philadelphia. He begged her to come down for a weekend visit, and eventually she acquiesced.

Her drive to Philly was ice cream and cookies until she hit the five o'clock rush. If you've ever driven the internal super highways at that time of day, you know what I mean. There's a series of intersections designed just for your driving displeasure, where three lanes are forced to meld with three others. Then you come to an intersection where two lanes on your left and one on your right are supposed to merge with yours. They have a similar situation in Rochester, New York, that locals call "The Can of Worms." I don't know what the locals call this driving nightmare, but I call it "Body Shop Heaven."

It doesn't actually help that these intersections are manned by police officers. Standing in the middle of the various intersections, motioning frantically for everyone to move their asses faster, they only have one objective—clear today's traffic. They don't care that you're pooping your pants going 45 to 50 mph, bumper to bumper, playing dodge'em cars and dodge'em cops through intersections copiously marked "Speed Limit 30 Strictly Enforced."

This was Alicia's situation when one of her front tires blew. Naturally, she pulled to a stop. Naturally, the nearest cop bellowed, "You can't leave it there lady, move it or lose it!"

She didn't know what to do. Cars zipped up behind her, honked furiously and swerved past, blessing her with copious cuss words and crude gestures.

As the cop started sauntering over to her, she began to cry.

"You've got to move it, lady!"

"I'm-supposed-to-meet-my-boyfriend, sob, sob, but-he's-in-school-and, sob, sob, I-don't-know-what-to, sob, sob, do-and if-I-try-to-drive, sob, sob, all-these-crazy-drivers-are-going-to, sob, sob, kill-me.

"I can't help that lady, but you've got to move it."

Sobbing even more, she cried, "All-your-license-plates-say 'You've Got a F-F-Friend in P-P-Pennsylvania', sob, sob, w-w-where's m-m-my f-f-friend?"

The cop changed the tire on the spot.

Continental Drifter

1. Clown of Thorns

Hello,

   We are having a nice visit here in Tucson with my cousin Dan and his wife Claudia at their beautiful new home. They had a meeting with their realtor this morning at their old house, which they're selling. While they were out, Art answered a couple of phone calls about problems that had to be reconciled before the sale could go through. They didn't take their cell phones with them so he decided to walk across the patch of desert that separates the two houses, rather than drive the car the long way around on the paved roads.

   Now, I know sometimes you guys think we make this stuff up, so I am going to let Cousin Dan tell the rest of the story.

   Love,

   Starr

Hi, All:

   My wife Claudia and I have laughed with the rest of you at the Arturo Saga series of stories Art and Starr have been emailing on their travels. Little did we know we would witness a Saga, much less become part of one to boot! So watch out; if you're within a block of my crazy cousin or her just-as-crazy husband, you too might become a character in a Saga of theirs.

   So, there Claudia and I are this morning in the house we're trying to sell, talking with our realtor. One of the contractors stops by for his money, but when I go to pay him, I realize I left my checkbook at our other house across the lot, which is a quarter mile away by car, but only 100 yards away by foot. So, the contractor and I decide to take the shortcut.

   As we walk through the front door, we see the swaying rear-end of an elderly man as he pulls himself up off of the desert floor. My first thought is he's some homeless guy who has wandered onto our property and napped for a while on the ground. Then this old guy turns a bit and I realize… it's Art!

What on Earth, I wonder to myself, is Art doing in the desert? When we left home half an hour ago, he was reading and Starr was thinking she might lie down for a nap. Why on Earth would he be hiking across the desert?

"Two…messages… from…contractors… about…house!" he yells to me, as he moves closer, hobbling over uneven ground. As he gets closer, I notice he has cactus needles on the front of his jacket. Then he hands me the messages, and I notice he also has cactus needles on the front of his pants. On the way back inside I notice he has cactus needles all over the back of his pants, too. And finally, when I introduce him to the contractor, I see cactus needles covering the backs of his hands. Ouch.

I give the messages to our realtor to handle. He and the contractor take this as their cue to get the heck out of Dodge — which they do very quickly, dust clouds billowing in their wake.

Soon, Claudia, Art and I are standing in the kitchen of this big, empty house, wondering what to do next. I decide to rush home and get tweezers and pliers, so the three of us can tackle the needles.

I take the truck…NO WAY am I going anywhere near that cacti-filled desert on foot! In four minutes I get home and tell Starr, who is trying to nap, that we're still at the old house. Art is with us, and the three of us will be back shortly. NO WAY am I going to tell her that Art, in strolling a few feet into the desert, had single-handedly lost a battle with a forest of man-eating cacti. Back I go to the vacant house with two pairs of pliers and two pairs of tweezers.

Let the games begin!

Claudia and I, with Art helping as best he can, remove needles from his jacket, his pants, and his hands. After ten minutes, we're making significant progress: Art can take off his jacket without being skewered by the needles inside. Hooray! Then we notice that there are more needles that have gone through his jacket and are embedded in his shirt. Gently, ever so gently, Art removes his shirt and…Hooray! There are no needles in his upper torso!

We're making great progress—or so we think—just a few needles in his left hand and a bunch on the back of his pant-legs to go. We work another 10 minutes and get most of the needles out of his pants.

But he's still feeling the jabs.

After some discussion, he and I conclude that there are more needles embedded in his lower left leg.

Claudia, who has been removing needles by the thousands from the seat of Art's pants, concludes that he must have a bunch of them in his arse, too.

Shite! What now, I wonder!

Claudia, who sometimes panics in an emergency, stays calm.

"Art," she commands, "drop your pants."

In about five seconds, Art is standing bare-ass naked, as ordered. Shite, I say to myself again, he sure dropped those pants fast enough. Let me interject here that I've always wanted Claudia to whisper in my ear, "Daniel, drop your pants!" I even practiced dropping them when I was younger, and I knew I could do it in about ten seconds. As I got older, my time increased, so now, at age 65, it takes me a good 20 seconds to get them off, and that's on a good day. Yet, here's Art, my senior by a dozen years, easily dropping trou in five seconds or less. What a stud!

Claudia now realizes that there are indeed needles well sunk in Art's butt and concludes that she sure isn't going to be the one to extract them. Mustering her calm once again, she quietly retrieves Art's pants from the floor, steps across the room and starts de-needling them.

"Can you work on his butt, Dan?" She asks with a smirk. Well, Art can't ride naked in the truck to have Starr do it. And we can't put his pants back on him with needles still in them. So, I figure I've drawn the short cactus needle… I get to work.

After some time, I finish with his backside and ask him to turn around so I can do his front. I've had better ideas. Suddenly, there I am on my knees with Art standing naked in front of me in the empty kitchen of a curtainless house. If one of those contractors or *a neighbor should just happen to stop by and just happen to look in the window...well... I've drawn you a clear enough picture, I think.*

Art diplomatically suggests that he can take it from here.

I thank Heavens and accept his kind offer.

The second Claudia sees what a daunting task un-needling his pants is, she decides to go to the new house and get Art another pair. Ha-ha! Now she gets to explain to Starr what's happening. I'm thrilled to be off that hook!

When Art and I are alone, we chat like two blind men in a nursing home, totally unmindful of the fact that one of us is naked as the proverbial jaybird. I wonder briefly if Art would feel more at ease if I took my clothes off, too. Nah, I decide, forget that! I'm not so sure I could remain so, um... relaxed... if the situation were reversed.

Soon, we're all back home, fully dressed, laughing, and telling Starr all about our Saga-worthy adventure. Now that's a day I will always remember and Arturo will probably never forget. At least, not when he tries to sit down!

Hello fans,

Arturo on the podium now —

I had really looked forward to visiting Starr's cousin Dan and his wife, Claudia, and we've all enjoyed getting to know each other better — although I get the feeling they'll be needling me about this little episode for years to come. Ah well, "sew" it goes.

Ouch! Now, where did I put those tweezers?

2. Geographically Challenged

F ew things can more confuse more things than can directions. Except the preceding sentence.

Take the for-instance where you're in a strange town looking for a certain street, as your wife keeps up a constant, "Why don't you ask somebody why don't you ask somebody why don't you ask—there: *that* man! You could have asked *him*. Here's a store! Pull over here." She doesn't realize that you don't ask because you know it won't do any good—and because you're a man, and men don't eat beige food, ask directions or run out of gas, ever, or almost ever, usually.

And, being a man, you also know it will do no good to ask "that man, there," because—being a man hims*elf*—he'll tell you exactly where it is, whether he knows or not. So you'll get directions like "Follow this road til it sort of veers off to the left; then you swoop around till you come to the old ball-bearing plant." (He neglects to tell you the plant's been closed for *ump* years, and the sign for it has been missing for *teen* years.) "Then you take the winding road through the park—but don't take any of the side roads, although you really can't tell they're side roads until you end up in the tennis court or on third base, or something..."

Years ago, Starr and I couldn't find the street in Scotia, New York, where a girlfriend of hers lived, so we stopped at a tavern. Before you ask, no, we didn't expect to find the street inside the tavern, but it was possible that someone inside might be able to guide us. (In manspeak, this is not "asking directions," it's "having a conversation.") Besides, we're just not in the habit of passing up taverns whenever we can help otherwise; we feel that would be downright antisocial. By the same token, it's not polite to just whip in and start asking directions—I mean, start up a conversation. Accordingly, we had a couple of drinks each as we made ourselves acquainted with our seatmates at the bar. One of those—a fellow named Sam Maritan—was pleased to "discuss local geography" with us. He seemed to know the area quite well, but his manner of speaking had us wondering if he was a retired traffic cop, or maybe a driving instructor.

"Go down to the stop sign on the corner," he said. "And *do* stop for it, because there's often a cop waiting for anyone who doesn't...So, you *will* stop for it!" Thereafter, everything he said sounded like a pronouncement from the highest office of the Third Reich. "You will come to an intersection and you will turn right!" To this day, Starr and I often give each other directions in command mode, reminiscent of our friend the Ubermeister of Scotia.

Anyway, directions confuse me—or maybe it's just the vocabulary. I know that an "east wind" and a "wind blowing west" are not opposites; they're the same thing. But if you add "-erly" (as in "easterly"), you've changed the wind's direction 180°. And somehow, New England became known as "Down East." How did that come about? Must have been named by an idiot Inuit. Besides, it's all relative, the Far East is the Near West to the Chinese, isn't it? And if South Carolinians are from the Deep South, how about Floridians, or people who live in Punta Arenas, the world's southernmost city?

And, oh yeah! Just where the heck is this Midwest that I'm supposed to live in? California is in the West, (actually it's in another dimension). But if that's so, then is Pennsylvania in the Near West? After all, when Soule (not Greeley) said, "Go west, young man!" he was referring to Buffalo, New York!

To get to Buffalo, you *must* go out the door; you will take an immediate left and open your car door. After that, you will be on your own. If you get lost on the way—I mean, if you get to exploring the countryside—*do* stop in a local tavern for a conversation. You won't get very good directions, but that's no reason to be anti-social, now is it?

3. Late for Dinner

"**Y**ou're late!" My new neighbor huffed.

She seemed awfully angry. Was I to blame? It was obviously just a slight regional difference. I had run into it before. Back East we ate at six or later, but here in the Midwest they usually ate a bit earlier. Since it was a quarter to six, I was late, but only forty-five minutes or so. And for this, I apologized.

"Forty-five minutes or so?" she exploded. "Try six hours! I invited you for dinner."

"And here I am," I said with a smile.

"Dinner is served at *noon!*"

Suddenly, I was transported back to my youth. Before I went to kindergarten, we had supper at six—and dinnertime *was* at noon! Once I started going to school, that changed. There, they called the midday meal "lunch" (probably because it was eaten in the lunch room). And the evening meal was called dinner and supper, though rarely both at the same time.

Soon my family and I stopped calling it dinner, and started calling it lunch like everybody else in town. Well, almost everybody. Mom alone continued to call lunch "dinner" and dinner, "supper." She was full-blooded German, you see; and self-admittedly true to stereotype, she was stubborn, very stubborn—uber-stubborn, you might say, which I just did, and she was given to being right, always. Just like me. I'm sure of it. And so are you. *Sieg heil!*

For the rest of us, lunch was lunch, and supper and dinner weren't.

Speaking of a meal that isn't, there is no such thing as "brunch"—never has been. Go to one and see. They have plenty of breakfast foods—omelets, bacon, sausage, waffles—but then they skip the usual luncheon fare like soup and sammiches, and go right to traditional supper stuff like hot roast beef, roasted chicken, mashed potatoes with gravy, and pies and cakes. That's not brunch—that's brupper!

And that sweet liquid in a bottle? That's not pop; it's soda. Pop is what the weasel goes.

And speaking of sweet, what is this Sweetest Day they celebrate here in Michigan? I already get in enough trouble for forgetting one Valentine's Day; why the frack do I need another one to forget? I really wish you guys had waited till I got here before you allowed that day to be declared. I would have flown a plane along Michigan Ave pulling a banner emblazoned with *Sweetest Day is the Hallmark of a Capitalist Plot.*

For the record, every Michigan town seems to have a Michigan Ave. Jackson, of course, has one, and it runs right through the middle of town. Apparently, they ran out of names when they got to the outskirts of town, because just about half of the inbound roads are called Jackson Road. They all intersect with Michigan Ave. at various points throughout the city, so if you miss one, don't worry, another one will be along soon.

Speaking of street names, back in Syracuse there's a street that drives travelers wacky. One minute they're on Genesee Street, a major thoroughfare, and the next thing they know, they're on James Street, a secondary route. We always got a chuckle out of saving lost souls.

That experience, however, did not help me one bit the day I asked for directions in Hillsdale County, Michigan.

"Sure, glad to help you," said a native Michigander. "Turn left on Bunn Road-Bankers Road-Carpenter Road, then turn right on Bankers Road-Fisher Road-Bennet Road, then..."

"Wait a minute," said I. "You mean I take my first three lefts, and then three immediate rights? Sounds like I'll be going around in circles. I've been doing that just fine on my own." For the sake of my own sanity, I thanked him, ignoring the fact that he had listed two Bankers Roads. However, my own sanity did not thank me a short while later when I actually came to the corner of Bankers Road and Bankers Road.

I'm pretty sure it's Michigan-annigans like this gave us the term "square route."

"No, no!" Protesteth the Samaritan. "The first three names are all one road, it just changes names every couple of miles. Same thing with the second road."

This didn't discombobulate me. I hadn't really been all that combobulated to begin with. Hadn't I just seen Main Street in the heart of downtown Camden switch from North to South and back again, all in the same block? Must be fun for a new mailman. "Look at me! I'm a human pinball! Boing! Boing!"

New Yorkers refuse to believe there's really a place in Michigan with the lyrical appellation, Cement City. Penn-silly-vanians, however, would believe it in a Mennonite minute, what with all the oddball city names *that* state has. What's up with that, Penn-brothers (and sisters)? I mean, traveling on Route 30 alone you've got Bird-in-Hand and Blue Ball, then you go through Intercourse to get to Paradise.

Nuff said?

One thing is for sure: my wife Starr and I have found most people in Michigan are a lot friendlier than people in New York. Now, New Yawkers aren't as heartless as you've been led to believe. I know you've heard that when a guy collapses on a New York sidewalk, having a heart attack or something, people just step over him and keep walking. That might be true in New York City, but it's not like that in the whole state. Honest. In cities like Rochester, Buffalo, and Syracuse, we think treating someone like that is just plain rude. We always make sure to carefully step *around* a guy who's collapsed on the sidewalk. It's more genteel.

I lived in Adrian, Michigan, for several months and loved it. I nicknamed it City of Parks since the name Park City was already taken. Everyone there lives beside a park. It's part of their urban renewal plan. Anytime anyone drops anything larger than a postage stamp on the ground, the Department of Parks puts a fence around it, tosses in some grass seed and names it after some local yokel who made good.

Likewise, I've heard it claimed that Jackson County, Michigan, has more lakes than any other county in the country. Well of course it does! Any body of water bigger than a toy poodle's piddle puddle gets called a lake. And any moose path, by whim or fancy, is called a highway. Furthermore, State law states that if a body of water is more squarish than it is rectangularish, it must be dubbed Round Lake. There are thousands of them.

On Fat Tuesday, Midwestern bakeries sell tons of *pacvkis*, which are basically super-rich jelly doughnuts. And while I had never heard of pacvkis before, no one outside of Central New York has ever heard of half-moon cookies. A half-moon is a large, soft, slightly-domed sugar cookie. Half of the flat side gets iced with vanilla frosting and the other half is iced with chocolate; hence the name.

Another regional delicacy you won't find in the Midwest is the salt potato. In Central New York, however, no self-respecting clambake would consider itself complete without the "salts." Salt potatoes were originally culls that were too small to sell at market and were saved for seed. Then some shrewd farmer boiled them in Central New York's ubiquitous brine, thus proving that Syracusans have a lot of salt.

My son claims he heard that the workers in the salt wells were often paid in potatoes, a staple in their diet. As part of the mining process, they infused water into the salt beds, pumped it back out, and then boiled it in huge vats until all the water evaporated leaving the salt behind. The salt miners would toss their small potatoes into the brine in the late morning and have boiled, salty spuds to munch on by lunch time.

When dipped in melted butter, they are delicious. (The salts, not the miners.)

I figure Michiganders don't know about salts because they don't have clambakes, as far as I can tell. And, boy! They don't know what they're missing, as far as they can tell.

At this point, I pause to make a few saline points...

Did you know that salt comes in lots because of Lot's wife?

She really turned out to be a pillar of society, didn't she?

Or that Syracuse's nickname is The Salt City? That's because the name City of Salt was already taken. Heck, the main road in Syracuse is named Salina Street—but not because the name Street of Salina was already taken. Salina Street just sounded better.

Salt, as every Central New York school child will tell you, was invented by a Jesuit priest, Pere LeMoyne, who Christianized and civilized the local Indians before they killed him. Look, don't ask me—that's what the nuns taught me. I just thought that if he was a better civilizer, they might not have done him in. But the nuns just thought that I was a smart ass. Ditto, when I asked, "Can God do anything?" The answer, of course, was that God is all-powerful. Which led to my follow-up question, "Can He make a rock so big He can't lift it?"

I remember seeing a Western show years ago that always ended with the line, "It happened that way, moving West." In one episode, a man who owned the only salt deposits in the area was murdered when he refused his neighbors access to it. Because salt was necessary for preserving food and therefore vital to life, they were all found "not guilty." How's that for pouring salt in the wound?

In conclusion, allow me to say my greatest culture shock in Michigan was my first alleged Coney Dog. "Now wait a minute," sez I. "I know what a Coney is, and it ain't no Red Hot with mustard and onion." You see, in Central New York, a Coney is shaped like a regular old hot dog, but its meat is white and it's spiced quite differently. Its closest cousin would be a bockwurst. I guess the German sausage makers skipped over Michigan when they were settling the land.

Well, that's all for now. Starr said we would be eating at three, and I sure don't wanna be late for lupper. Sunch? Whatever!

4. Easy as Ah, Bay, Say

If you're going to live in Mexico, you absolutely must learn Spanish.

Any good language teacher will tell you the first rule in learning a language is to learn the vowels. And in the Spanish language, the vowels are legion—why have five vowels when you can have nine? That's right, *nine*. And they are, in no particular order: A, E, I, O, U, Y, LL, EH and AH. So, now you know—which goes to show you that I am not just a good language teacher, I am a *mucho goodo* language teacher.

When standing alone, "e" and "y" mean "and." So in those instances they give up their original classifications as vowels and become full-fledged words.

To pronounce a Spanish "e" you say an English "a"—but to pronounce a Spanish "a" you do not say an English "e." You open wide and say "ah." That's because you have to reserve the English "e" sound to make the Spanish "i" sound. Is that all as clear as mud now?

To get you to pronounce "u" properly, I must first tell you a little story.

My youngest daughter's youngest daughter was much younger than her two elder sisters. When the older girls were much younger, my youngest daughter and my son-in-law did not hide their bodies when nude. I guess it was a sort of a 'coming attractions' approach to Sex Ed. However, as the two older girls got older it was decided that more privacy was in order, so by the time their youngest came along everyone was in the habit of covering up, including my son-in-law. As a result, his youngest daughter had never seen him naked.

One day, just as my son-in-law was stepping out of the shower, his youngest daughter who was now about five, came through the bathroom door bent on telling him something very important. As she burst in, her eyes took a fast southern tour. Shocked and apparently disgusted, she let out a loud, protracted, "Yeeeeew!"

And that is exactly how you pronounce a Spanish "u."

Now we need to pay attention to a few consonants.

"J," and "g," if it happens to come before an "e" or an "i," when properly pronounced, sounds like you're trying to hack up a hairball. As a result, "j," "g," and sometimes "x" all take the place of "h," so there really doesn't seem to be a need for "h" at all. Therefore you can just toss the "h" the H outta here, especially since everyone else here does.

A double "l" is pronounced like an English "y."

"Z" is pronounced like an English "s." So if they really, really wanted to, they could get rid of S, Y, X, H and G, and streamline typesetting overnight. Not to mention how much simpler it would make the job of a very good Spanish teacher such as myself. But they really, really don't want to.

There is one more salient point that should be explored and this is it: why do Tijuanans pronounce "Tijuana" as "TiaQuana"? Pay attention and you'll hear that tiny clicking sound when they say it. What's that all about?

Unnondisirregardless of these little inconsistencies, all of the forgoing musings really don't mean spit. For, as any Mazatlico will tell you, we non-Mazatlicos cobble all sorts of words together to make up new words that nobody else in Mexicolandia can understand, anyway.

As I see it, it's all the fault of the Conquistadores, who had no business speaking a "romance language" in the first place. Something Germanic—like English—would have suited their temperament so much better. In Germanic languages, if you need a word that doesn't exist yet, you build it from ones that do. That way when you say "gebietstehendbaum," everyone knows you mean in-the-field-standing-tree. See? Simple as ein, swei, drei...

5. Horace Greeley Said...

"*G*o North, Young Man, Go North."

My lexicographer said, "No, he didn't. But he didn't say 'west' either; John L. B. Soule did." But the three men I admire most—my urologist, cardiologist and ophthalmologist—all told me to go north. So off I flew, north by north-north, to their offices in Dallas.

"Art, you idiot," you say. "Texas is in the South." Well, Texas may not seem northerly to those from The States, but it's way north if you go by way of Mazatlan, Mexico.

The first day, my ophthalmologist peeled my left eye.

The next day, the urologist violated my sanctum sanctorum and actually gave me good news, declaring that my body could no longer be an official stop on the annual Easter egg hunt because the new wonder drugs that I was on had shrunk my egg-sized prostate to the size of a peanut, and nobody wants a peanut-sized prostate in their Easter basket.

A couple of days later the cardiologist Roto-Rootered my right leg.

Then the ophthalmologist scraped my right eye.

Not to be outdone, the cardiologist said he wanted seconds too and scheduled a return visit in September.

With that, they all declared I was good for another 25,000 miles.

Beyond that good news, by lumping their visits together, I paid only one deductible and saw the men I trust. Besides, the doctors in Mexico don't dig my humor. They just look at me the way George Burns looked at Gracie Allen when it was time to say goodnight.

Those savings were easily canceled out by the airfare, of course. We had to pay even more than usual, because I changed my flight and went two weeks earlier than planned. And while we're on the subject, how come when I hop on a bus, even a Grey-hound, I pay the same fare every time—but air fares go up and down? What's next? "Welcome to See-Saw Air. Your airfare was based on having a full plane. The plane is only half full so you will have to pony up more before we can land."

While we were in Texas, we began the process of selling our homestead of twelve years in Big D. We interviewed several real-tors and found one to our liking who gave us an estimated asking price. We knew from experience that we could drive the asking price up if we did some repairs and cosmetic work on the place, so Starr and I worked our heinies off prepping the house for sale. We polished, cleaned and painted. Arranged for tradesmen where needed. Got electric, pool and lawn service. Made a deal with an estate sales organization to sell the furnishings. Called a charity to pick up whatever didn't sell. Then we called the realtor, who said just one word: "Wow!" And raised her offering price by eight thousand dollars.

We got to see many of our friends in Dallas, and I shot some pool with my old teammates. Jeff and Cindy put us up (and put up with us) for three weeks—we even got to play Euchre with them. The girls did their best, but the team of Jeff and Art were just too tough for Cindy and Starr. At the end of three weeks, they were so glad to see us go, they threw a party.

Due to the aforementioned last-minute rescheduling, our return flights had Starr leaving from Love Field and me flying out of DFW.

Only forty-two years together and people are already saying, "I told you that marriage would never last."

6. Weisenheimer's Disease

"**Y**ou never listen!" says my liebfrau.

It's not true, of course—I do listen. The problem is that she goes on at such great length, and so damned often, and with so much boring detail. And she does it when I'm trying to read the latest historical novel, or shoot a game of pool, or watch my third or fourth game on Sunday television, making it impossible to catch or remember much at all, much less every little detail.

You aren't going to believe this, but my leapenfrog was convinced that my inability to remember her every blessed word was because I had Altzenhausers. So just to prove her wrong—and to get a little rest for my ears—I made an appointment with my GP.

Der Liebfraumilch insisted on coming along.

"What the hell! Don't you trust me to tell you what he says?" asked I from my dudgeon on high.

"Oh, I trust you," she says, donning her best huff. "I trust you to forget half of what he says, either because you have Old-timer's, or more likely, because YOU JUST DON'T LISTEN! You turn here."

"Where?"

"If you're going to the doctor's, you turn back there."

You see how bad it's getting? She makes such a big deal about my missing that stupid turn, like it proves her point about Applesauzer's disease. She knows damn well I always miss that turn. I've lived in this city for over seventy years, and I've always missed that turn.

To make matters worse, when we finally get to the doctor's, doesn't he have to be in one of his really pissy moods? He starts bitching me out for being late. Now let me ask you, when was the last time you went to a doctor and actually got to meet face to face with him within forty-five minutes of the alleged appointment?

And did you bitch him out? Oh, no! We're all too chicken to do that; even for us agnostics there are still some high priests. But here he is, on my case—and he's wrong.

I tell him so.

"My appointment was for three, and I was here at three."

"I'm not talking about the hour," he retorts. "I'm talking about the day. You were supposed to be here yesterday!"

I could see it wasn't worth prolonging the argument, but like I told my wife on the way home, "If you ask me, it's our doctor who's suffering from Axlehammer's. I couldn't have had an appointment with him yesterday; everybody knows doctors play golf on Thursday." She mumbled something about today being Saturday. I thought for a minute she was going to pick up on my mention of Axandhammer's and start that crap again—and so help me, if she did, I swore I would pop her one, to the Moon, Alice, to the Moon—but, for once, she let it be.

Anyway, while we were there, the doctor asked me about my drinking.

"Oh, you know, I enjoy a couple when I get home from work."

Doesn't La Boca Grande have to stick her two cents in with "You retired four years ago."

So he pressed me, and I finally told him that I got drunk, oh maybe, two, three nights a week—Hey, I'm no different than you; if I told him the truth, he'd probably faint.

Didn't much matter, he still wanted me to join the Club. That's when it hit me why Miss Slippery-Shoes wanted to come along. She probably called him and suggested that I needed professional help; that my drinking was giving me Alcohoheimer's disease.

I knew the only way I was going to get these two harpsichords off my back was to go along with them...for a while. So I went to a meeting.

Wow, what an experience! First of all, there were all these grubby guys in dirty greasy clothes. It isn't at all like in the movies, where Jeff Bridges calmly stands up and everyone rivets their attention on him, while he says, "My name is such-and-such. I am an alcoholic." Oh no, at a real meeting, everybody's attention is riveted on themselves, except the one guy who wants to be first to confess. His face looked like his nose had a duel with a pneumatic drill—and lost.

Finally, one guy does get the floor, and says, "My name is Chuck Fenders. All my friends call me Bender. For years I wouldn't listen when my wife and friends tried to tell me, but finally, I had to face it. I was firing on about one-and-a-half cylinders, if you know what I mean, and, man, I tell you, I needed to make a pit stop or things were going to take a left turn real quick. I couldn't pass a garage without being lured in. The wife would send my son, Chip, or my daughter, Scratch, to plead with me to come home, and I'd promise to. I really meant to. But until those pumps were shut down, the last bit of ethanol poured and the lights turned out, I couldn't leave. The next day it would happen all over again. For me, one ball-joint is too many and a thousand are not enough. My name is Benders Fenders and I...I'm an auto mechanic."

At this point, Old Lightningflak comes storm-trooping into the meeting, pulls me out the door and deposits me in the passenger seat of the car. "You old fool," she admonishes as she pulls out into traffic and starts our cross-city trek, "you're supposed to be at the AA meeting, not the AAA meeting. The pilots and doctors are pulling their hair out, waiting for you. And all because YOU JUST DON'T LISTEN!"

"Yes dear," I calmly replied, not daring to mention she'd just missed our turn.

7. In-Continental Breakfast

*O*n a recent visit to the Sunshine State, Starr and I closed the bar we'd been exercising our Squatters' Rights in for the better part of a Friday evening and, along with our friend Ron, went looking for something to eat.

Unfortunately, everywhere we went was closed. So, we drove hungrily along looking for someplace—any place—to eat, when finally, after six or seven hundred miles, we found a place that was open.

It was a cavernous tavern but there was only one occupied table in the whole place.

Now, as you know, Starr and I were restaurateurs in a former life and as such we should have known enough to turn around and walk right back out. But we didn't. Probably because, as Joe Bonamo said years ago in so many words, "Appetite is selective; hunger eats anything." Besides, there were three other things that stopped us: we didn't know the area, we had already driven the aforementioned six or seven hundred miles to find this place, and when Ron is hungry you don't stand between him and his fork—well, not unless you wanted your face to look like a pack of pissed-off porcupines had gone to town on it, you didn't. Anyway, the point is, an almost-empty restaurant on a Friday night does not bode well for the discerning, or even the not-so-discerning, diner.

The waitress greeted us at the door. "Smoking or non-smoking?" she asked.

"Smoking," we answered.

"Follow me, please."

She led us across this very, very large establishment and, as she handed us menus, said, "I don't know why I asked that, y'all. At this time of night the whole place is smoking."

And that was the closest we were going to get to sanity for the rest of the evening.

When she came back to take our order, she brought some, ahem, rolls. They looked more like those fake pastries you find cowering in glass cases in greasy spoon diners all across America. But instead of being made of foam, these delicacies were made of rock. Rock that had been painted to look like rolls, but rock nonetheless. I know this is true because when one of these thunder-rolls rumbled off the table, it broke my big toe—causing this little piggy to go *wah-wah-wah* all the way home.

Having noticed our waitress sported a Texas drawl, and since Starr and I had once lived in Texas, I asked her where she was from. She named the town and went on her merry way. Starr said, "I know the town. It's four corners in the middle of nowhere whose only claim to fame is a combination ice cream stand bait shop."

At this point things really began to pick up. In a matter of only thirty or forty or fifty minutes, give or take an hour, our Texas-drawling waitress brought me my breakfast. I subtly mentioned I hadn't ordered an omelette, I'd asked for scrambled eggs. The waitress didn't have a clue what the 'subtle' difference was. Obviously, the cook didn't either, because a few minutes later the waitress brought Starr a scrambled egg omelette of her very own.

Did I mention we were very, *very* hungry? We ate.

When Starr and I finished our food, we turned to ask Ron how his was, but thought the better of it when we noticed he still hadn't been served. That's right: the poor man still hadn't been given a single thing to eat except boulder rolls! He had, however, been given a fork—a fork he was waving wildly about, stabbing at the air in a most unsettling, porcupine-with-an-icepick manner.

Miss Texas brought Ron's food at long last, and then returned shortly to ask him how his breakfast was.

"Well, Miss, I ordered my eggs over light. So, what light did they cook them over? A blowtorch? These eggs are so hard they aren't fit for prison food! You'd have to put them in a vice to get these yolks to run."

She reached for his plate. "I'll have the cook fry two more."

Ron flung both arms flat out on the table, surrounding his plate, exclaiming, "No! I can't wait another hour. I just want to eat and go to bed."

An hour or two later, she brought the bill. I looked it over, reached into my pocket and pulled out a twenty. She took it to the register, but after a moment came back to the table and wanted to know if I had anything smaller. I said no.

As she walked away again, Starr noted my dumbfounded expression and asked, "How much was the bill?"

"Sixteen seventy-five."

Starr giggled mischievously. "Take back the twenty and give her two fives. See what she does with *that*."

Just before we left, Miss Ice-Cream-Stand-and-Bait-Shop floated by the table and asked, "Anything else?"

Ron looked up and said, "Yes, ma'am, the name of a good restaurant."

Our heroine paused for a second, looked down at Ron and, as if any sense of irony had been ironed out of her long ago—if, indeed, there had *ever* been any sense in her, ironical or other-wise—she drawled, "wall, y'all, there's a Denny's, but it's a real pain goin' down there 'cause they're usually pretty packed about now, 'specially on the weekend. Y'all have a nice night now, y'hear?"

Starr and I have never been so grateful to eat in a Denny's as we were the next night.

Ron stayed behind and dined al fresco at Casa De Vending Machine in the hotel lobby.

8. Las Vegas, Nirvana

First time in Vegas.

One whole week of playing seven card stud, shooting craps, losing my stake, staying up all night, getting crap from Starr for shooting craps, losing my stake, and always being too tired to go see the Who-Gives-a-Hoover-Dam or the lake the Indians know as Lake Mead which is how everyone else knows it, too, since it didn't exist until a relatively short time ago, so there is no Indian name for it but if there were, it might be Lake Wheredidallthe-fishingo, or maybe Lake Flaccid. Honestly, it looks like a puddle of warm spit, smack dab in the middle of a desolate, forbidding moonscape.

Please forgive the run-on sentences, the redundancies and the run-on sentences. But if you've ever been to Vegas, you probably know where I'm coming from—life in Vegas *is* a run-on sentence. The place never shuts down—or shuts up for that matter. Whenever I'm there, I hear a constant whisper in my ear that I just can't resist. "Hey, Art, go ahead and play one of the tables. It's what you came here for, right?" And I always answer, "Right!" And then I chuckle low to myself, heh-heh. Because what the Irresistible Voice doesn't know is...I've got a system. That's right. I've got a system. So take that, you City of Broken Dreams! I swear by all that is holy and much that is not, those casinos won't know what hit 'em when I'm through with them! Bwahahahaha!

All I have to do is work out a few bugs...

That part of Las Vegas Boulevard known as "The Strip" is about fifty roulette tables wide, and filled with a zillion cars—all driven by losers who, too cowardly to take their own lives, are out to take yours. You realize this at about the same time you realize you're driving on the median, and that one way or another—most probably another—you must plunge back into traffic because the crap shoot is not over. You've got to do it all over again on the next block...and the next...and the next.

Contrary to rumors spread by Binion, the streets in Vegas are not paved with gold. The sides of the streets are paved with gold, because that's where the casinos are. The streets themselves are paved just like the streets in New Yawk City—with slow pedestrians.

My first time out, I wondered who the parade was for that left so much confetti strewn about the streets and sidewalks. Closer inspection revealed that, au contrare, mon frère, it wasn't confetti covering the city like a blanket of new-fallen volcanic ash—It was ripped-up Keno slips and pawn tickets.

When you return home from Vegas, the first thing people will ask you is "Did you win?"

The only answer for this is, "I was there for a week."

Unless you only stay for a couple of hours, why in God's name would anyone think you could win? You probably have a better chance of going to the moon or winning the state lottery. And recently, I heard some statistic-savant say that you have a better chance of getting struck by lightning than you have of hitting the Lotto.

Let me explain the facts of life to you. Property on The Strip costs $5,000 a square foot. The Mirage Casino has mountains, volcanoes, waterfalls, jungles, and white tigers in such a spacious, gorgeous and, I presume, climatically realistic habitat that the felines in Syracuse's Burnet Park Zoo would gladly give their two front canines to trade places with them.

And this is just the park you walk through to get to the casino. We still haven't gotten to the casino proper, which is just one casino out of about a quadrillion and ninety-two.

So if you're walking through a Caesar's, a Bally's, or say, an Imperial, and you're wondering who paid for all of this, the only answer is, "I was here for a week."

People who ask such a silly questions as "Did you win?"—who somehow think the investors invested truckloads of cash just so peons like you and me can go home with more banana chips in our pockets than we had when we got there—should never go to Vegas. Their silly questions would drown out the irresistible Voice of Las Vegas, and they'll never win that way.

What they need is a system...

9. Mañana Never Comes

They say living is easy down south of *The South*,
The seafood's so fresh it just melts your mouth.
So they come for a visit, and they think that it's quaint,
But the folks here who live it have found that it ain't.
It's true that it's cheaper to buy a new home,
But mail from the States seems to come via Rome.
If I hire a tradesman to work on my place,
He'll promise, "Mañana!" with a grin on his face,
Then arrive three days later. But ask him, "Porque?"
And he'll say "Mañana's tomorrow...and that's not today"

I implored them to hook up my condo's electric
In under a week, and they called me eccentric.
I rang up my banker, I phoned Immigration,
But found the whole system imbued with stagnation.
My calls went unanswered, I started to weep,
I'd forgotten siesta! The whole town's asleep!
But nothing will change despite all my tears,
For that's how they've done things for thousands of years.
Vendrá cuando venga*, as the old-timers say,
Mañana's tomorrow...it's never today

* *He'll come when he comes*

10. Mexico is (Not) a Third World Country

Mexico is not a Third World country, and it is definitely not a Second World country, whatever that is. No, mis amigos, Mexico is a world of its own. And if you want to avoid hypertension, you quickly learn to slow with the flow that is Old Mexico.

Shortly after moving to the seaside city of Mazatlan, my wife and I set out one morning to do all the stuff that always comes with moving into a new place. We had a huge list, with "open a checking account" in first place. Starr tossed the last load of wash into the dryer and off we went.

We were met by the Official Bank Greeter, whose sole job was funneling people into the correct line. We told him we wanted to open an account. "The Bank Clerk line is over there, *por favor,*" he helpfully replied.

So we got in the Bank Clerk line, and slowly moved up to the counter where the Bank Clerk smiled and said, "To open an account, take a number from the ticket dispenser over there by the Official Bank Greeter and wait for your number to come up on the Bank Officer Screen."

Ay, caramba! Already it was clear that the employees here did not play well with each other—and that never bodes well for the customers.

We danced a few more rounds of the Bureaucratic Shuffle until we finally got to sit down with an Official Bank Officer who, between phone calls, faxes and the occasional sip of cafe, informed us that we lacked our FM3 Proof of Non-Citizenship Forms from the Passport Office. She helpfully jotted down the address along with some illegible directions, and sent us on our way.

Dios mio! The Passport Office was on the other side of the friggin' city! Okay, it's not a huge city—but it's hot and it's crowded and it takes forever to crawl up and down the main thoroughfare.

At this point, I want you to sit back, relax, and imagine that your Magic Eight Ball has rolled "Anything Is Possible."

Okay, ready? Here we go.

We drove through barrio after barrio, and suddenly (cue "Twilight Zone" music), we entered a world out of time—a land of wall-to-wall people and cars, with not a single one moving.

And then we saw why. A parade.

Yup, that's right, a parade. A lovely, multicolored pageant of pomp and poverty, with blaring horns (both automotive and musical), dancing senoritas and festive floats piled miles high with feathers and flowers. Despite all this, the whole thing moved with a curious languor, oozing down the avenida like salsa mole, and blocking traffic for miles around.

We soon learned that such is the norm in Mexico. Did you know that "mexico" actually means "parade" in ancient Mayan? It does. So there's a parade for something or other every day of the week, and several on Sundays. Why? Because it's Mexico!

Even when there isn't a parade, there's plenty to slow you down on the streets of Mazatlan. At most traffic lights, you find windshield washers—young men trying to make a few bucks by honest work. We appreciate that they're doing something of mutual benefit. Because of this, we usually tip them, even though our windshield was washed at the last red light and the light before that.

Sometimes you see miniature vaudeville acts like three guys tossing a girl in the air, or maybe two people juggling bowling pins. There's the flame-thrower guy who burns his lips one out of six times. (I hear he's up for a role in a Blistex ad.) But the grand-daddy of them all was the guy Starr saw juggling two oranges: even with only two orbs, he still dropped one half the time. On her way back home she arrived at his corner to find him juggling only one. Did he eat one? Did one roll under a car and get lost or squashed? No matter. Even with only *one* he kept dropping it!

We arrived at the Official Passport Office at precisely two-oh-two. You guessed it: they closed at two for siesta. Why?

Because it's Mexico!

The next day we were told by the kind young woman at the Official Passport Office that we would have to go home and bring back a piece of mail that had our address on it.

"But we just moved here, so we haven't been sent any mail," I whined.

"That's okay," she said. "Get someone else's mail—the landlord's, or a neighbor's."

"But it won't have our name on it *or* the right address."

"That's okay," she said again.

Silly me! Of course it was okay. What better proof of being a non-citizen could I have than a piece of mail with someone else's name and address on it?

While we were waiting there in the non-immigration office getting non-instructions on proving non-proof of non-citizenship by presenting non-personal-mail, we noticed a thumping noise in a back office.

I took a peek.

From what I could figure out, it seems it was one unfortunate employee's sole job to whack an ink stamp on an ink pad— whack!—and then whack stacks upon stacks of paper with the ink stamp. Whack, whack, whack, whack!

And they had a drill press (no lie!) in that selfsame back office, where it was some other poor soul's sole job to punch holes in the stacks and stacks of whacked paper, to prepare them for the three-ring binders that would bind them all.

Apparently, the Mexican Government loves lots and lots of copies of everything.

Apparently, the Mexican Government loves lots and lots of copies of everything.

Be that as it may, the Mexican penchant for duplication didn't help us in the least the time the bank couldn't find a land trust document that had been filed in their office only a week before.

Back for Round three, we returned with our non-letter, hoping against hope that now we could get our FM3's, and go to the bank to finish the first thing on our list—open a bank account.

"Gracias," the clerk said, smiling. "Now you must take all of these papers down the block to the Coca Cola stand..."

Yes, you read that right: a Coca-Cola stand.

"...where they will make sure your papers are in order and filled out correctly. Then you must bring them back here to this office and we'll make sure everything is in order. Then we'll give you a date to appear at the Official Notary's Office and have your signatures officially notarized."

"Anything else?" I muttered.

"Not really. Just bring everything back here when you're done there, and we'll make sure everything is in order, and you'll be all set."

Ay, ay, ay!

I bit my tongue, not asking if it would be alright for my neighbor to finish up for me since it was his identity we were using to prove we lived there but didn't live there.

Slowly but surely I was beginning to accept that this was a different culture than the one I was raised in. For instance, if a Norte Americano like me puts his house up for sale and it doesn't sell, he will probably lower the price. But if a Mexican puts his house up for sale and he gets no serious offers, he will probably raise the price, because, because...because it's Mexico!

And there's the owner of a local hamburger stand who bought some jumbo hotdogs in Sam's Club. He started selling them at his stand and was doing fabulously. Then, one day he went to Sam's Club and there were no more jumbo dogs on the shelves. After several dogged trips he asked the manager what happened to the big dogs. The manager said they kept selling out of them, so he quit ordering them from his supplier!

Why?

Don't ask questions. Just know this: in Mexican, "To Do List" translates into "Spin the Gringo."

On the way home, I turned to Starr and said, "Look at the bright side, honey, It took three trips but at least we got one thing done."

"And what was that?"

"That load of clothes you put in the drier before we left." I answered triumphantly.

And with that, we decided to hit the cantina to celebrate our one accomplishment of the day. But first, a nap. Because, you know...it's Mexico.

11. Michigan on the Alluvial Plain

*T*oday's lesson is on the proper use of the word "alluvial." You're not required to know what it means—just how to use it. Sort of like "antidisestablishmentarianism." Everybody knows that antidisestablishmentarianism is the longest non-medical word in the English dictionary, but how many can use antidisestablishmentarianism in a sentence, not counting sentences like this one?

And so it is with the word "alluvial."

You hear the word all the time, but who knows what it means? All we know for sure is that it's usually followed by the word "plain." Sort of like the way "drunken" is usually followed by "bum"—and "drunken bum" is usually followed by "Arturo."

That reminds me of a story. I had been in college about a year or so and I was, er, exploring life. Naturally, this worldly exploration meant that I was still living in my parent's home. (Hey, conquering the world one beer at a time is expensive!) One night I heard my mom and papa talking.

"Archie, I'm worried about Artie. I don't think he's learning a thing in college."

"Oh, I don't know, Edith—he's learned how to be a drunken bum."

"Well then, that's the only thing. And he's lazy, too, Archie. I've seen riverbed alluvium with more get-up-and-go than that boy of yours."

Well, to be fair, mom was kinda right. I was lazy and I was also a drunken bum. But that wasn't all I learned at college. I took my studies very seriously. I was learning all kinds of stuff, like how to be a lecher, a voyeur, a gambler, a philanderer, and a debaucher.

And I minored in Accounting, just in case.

It took me decades to master those skills, but master them I did (all except for the accounting). Until one day I realized it was time for greener pastures—pastures where all the other cowpokes didn't see me coming from a mile away. So I began to travel—and that's how I arrived here in the Alluvial West and the Great State of Michigan.

Wanna know how I know the Great State of Michigan is great? Because every politician who has ever campaigned here has proclaimed immediately upon their arrival, "My fellow Americans, I am proud to visit the Great State of Michigan!" And politicians wouldn't lie.

Not long after I got to the alluvial plains in the Great State of Michigan, I noticed a couple of things I thought were odd.

One: the people of the Great State of Michigan are car crazy. Every last one of them owns at least two classic cars — even the children—it's the law.

And, B: all of these collectible cars are driven day in and day out by their collective drivers over a vast collection of sand. Or the "Sand Spit," as the locals call it. The Vast Sand Spit of Michigan is alluvial. And by alluvial I mean flat, even though I'm pretty sure that's not what alluvial really means. The mean elevation is so low that it's only slightly higher than Floor-ida but not quite as low as Death Valley in...in...that other State. (Now you know why I failed as a geography teacher.)

Someday it's going to rain really, really hard on this alluvial plain and a zillion old cars are gonna slide very, very slowly into Lake Huron on the one side, and into Lake Michigan on the other. And it is my fervent hope that because of all those automobiles spilling into the drink, the Triple A Insurance Company will also slide off the face of the Alluvial West and go under, never to be seen again.

And yes, that is the same Triple A that tells you where to go and how to get there, just like many a mother-in-law. They're big players in the insurance game here—Triple A, not mothers-in-law. But the insurance game here is played very oddly indeed.

Then again, they play a lot of things oddly out here. Take

the Great American Game, for instance. Well, the bastard child of the great American game, anyway. No, not Wheel of Fortune. I'm talking about slow pitch baseball. Here in the Great State of Michigan, a slow pitch runner doesn't have to wait for the batter to make contact with the ball. He can leave a base on the swing of the bat. Try doing that in the Empire State of New York, I quadruple-dog-dare-you.

Want more? Okay! I stopped into a bar and asked if anyone would like to play pitch. An old timer with a big bushy beard and a hippie braid—which describes every adult male Michigander—said, "Well we've got a pit out back, but it's a bit cold to throw today, innit?"

"I didn't mean horseshoes, I meant a card game."

"Sounds like a sissy game to me. Here in the Great State of Michigan, we-uns play Euchre. You know: right bower, left bower, only cards above 8."

Want more? Take the great un-American pastime, according to the animal rights-ist: hunting. In Michigan, it's legal to bait animals, and many stores sell bulk bags of carrots, beets, and stuff like that for that purpose. In New York, however, the baiting game is against the law. Not that most folks in upstate New York (and I mean up-upstate New York, as in Brassie Corners, Whippleville and Chateauguay, not down-upstate New York, as in those hills just north of New York City) are aware they've been breaking the law all these years.

"What the f^%#?" they would ask in the politest of tones, if told. "Baiting is illegal? No way!"

Also, until I moved here, I never heard the name "Travis" that much, except for John D. MacDonald's colorful protagonist. But here, every seventh guy is a Travis, and they all sing, and they all twang on their guitars, and they all drive pick-up trucks.

That thar's ma house, Twang!

That thar's ma bride. Twang!

That ain't ma truck, Twang!

Parked in ma drive. Twang! Twang!

Or words to that defect.

Except, of course, on the days they're putt-putt-puttering around the Sand Spit in one of their big, obligatory classics.

If all of the foregoing seems odd, the auto insurance laws are, as I mentioned, even odder (even odder, how's that for an oxymoron?) Out here, they have something they call no-fault insurance. No. Fault. Insurance. (I ask once again, how's that for an oxy, moron?)

The Triple A insurance man explained it to me this way. "If you have an accident," he said, "*you* don't sue because your insurance company pays you, and the *other* person doesn't sue you because their insurance company pays them! It's 'no-fault' and that's the way it works. Unless you think that the other person is really, really at fault. Then you sue, but if you do sue and the judge finds out that the other person really, really isn't at fault, then you will have to pay court costs and the other person's lawyer's fees, because it's your fault if you say that someone who really, really isn't at fault really, really is at fault when there really, really is No Fault.

"Some liberal types awhile back," the agent added, "petitioned to change the law, but most of the folks in the Alluvial West are even more conservative than those rigid nineteenth-century Anglicans with their antidisestablishmentarianism. And we all know how that turned out, now, don't we?"

12. O Pissmas Tree

'Twas the week before Christmas and all thru the land
In each neighbor's window, a Yule tree did stand.
But ours had no yew, we had not been around,
When out by the curbing, a fake tree we found

I sprang from my car and rang on the bell,
"Is that for the taking? It is? Ain't that swell!"
Indoors my son took it the very next day,
Where he started to pull the dead light bulbs away

The going was slow, although the lad hastened—
Those tiny white lights were fastidiously fastened.
For many an hour the good fellow toiled,
'Til he smelled something funky, like diapers be-soiled

The branches, he realized, were reeking with pee,
Thus he Sherlocked the plight of the poor Pissmas Tree,
He said, "Folks on the lake have doggies named Spot,
There are deer, and some bears, and the goose we dubbed
    Dot

They all must have taken a nightly sojourn
To stand 'round this thing and deposit their ur'ne."
"The fates are against us!" mein hausfrau did grouse.
"Get it out of the house. *Raus mit em, raus!*"

So beware all you skinflints who shop by the road
Lest odoriferous odors befoul your abode,
Splurge on a spruce from a Christmas tree farm,
And celebrate free of olfactory harm!

13. Some Deserve to Die

*O*ur dog, Bob, was pissed off because he wasn't invited on our Hawaiian vacation. So he tried to cancel it by tripping me and breaking my wrist the day before our departure. At the hospital in Dallas they put on a temporary cast, with the admonishment that I must be sure to go to an orthopedist the next day.

BULLSHIT! I wasn't going to a doctor the next day—I was going to Maui.

Maui, where Pat Sajak couldn't charge me to take a vowel because they're scattered around in the language as freely as guano in a bat cave. Seeing as how "H" and "W" are already halfway to voweldom, if it weren't for the consonants "L" and "N," everybody in Hawaii would be speaking like they'd had seven shots of Jack Daniels and twelve of Novocain.

Upon our arrival, I tried to get an appointment with the only orthopedist on Maui, but the best I could do was to set one up for the last day of our vacation. I begged and pleaded with the receptionist. "C'mon," I whined. "It's my vacation of a lifetime. You know—water skiing, snorkeling and all of that."

Oh, well. I'd just have to settle for a two-week unguided tour of all the island's watering holes. We *did* have a fantastic mountaintop condo that Starr and I were sharing with my daughter Karen and my pseudo son-in-law Dogwood. Every morning Starr and I would walk down into the village and eat some gooey, sugary thing that would give our cardiologists angina. Then we'd claw our way back home. That road was actually steeper than the volcano road we almost ascended in our rental on Christmas Day, but didn't quite, due to the local gas station owner not having the foresight to remain open when tourists needed gas.

We traveled the island and saw all of the sights, which consisted of lava and more lava. I admit I was disappointed we didn't get to see the leprosarium on Molokai, but we actually made it up the road to Hana—a road that deserves its own bumper sticker. For the road to Hana is paved with tiny bridges—267 of them, give or take 500. And it comprises over a zillion hairpin curves—curves so sharp that the driver has to continually look out the side windows to see where the road goes next. Subsequently, the first building you see when entering either terminal city is a chiropractor's office offering a neck massage specialty.

At the end of our stay, I finally got to see the orthopedist, who put a waterproof cast on my wrist. "Now you can go swimming, snorkeling, and water skiing.

By the way, how long are you here for?" he asked.

"I leave in the morning," I mumbled.

"Uh, well, I hope you enjoyed your Hawaiian vacation."

And I hope you enjoy this nice Hawaiian punch!" I thought, but did not say...

14. State of Displacement

This winter Starr and I again made the ten-day hadj to the State of Displaced Persons, a.k.a. Florida. We carefully packed our cribbage board, fishing poles and a suitcase full of grade-22 sunscreen. This last item is the most essential one; without it, the backs of our hands would blister and peel from the strong rays emitted by the florescent lights of the many taverns we force each other to visit.

If you've never been to Florida, then you are the person I want to have reading this article. As a seasoned snow bird, with a solid background of over nineteen days, there are many invaluable (as opposed to valuable) things I have to impart, so that should you ever go, you'd fit right in and no one would ever know you weren't a native Floridian.

Actually, that's not so horribly difficult, because in truth, you have a better chance of seeing an alligator on Alligator Alley than you have of finding a native-born Floridian. The reason for this is that thirty years ago Florida had a total population of seven. This was back in the days when people knew that if you retired, you would be dead within a year. Everybody knew that. This was also—and I don't expect you younger readers to believe this— back in the days when college students spent the entire school year studying. But then sociology was invented and it provided us with some very interesting insights. Such as, if you shipped Gramma and Gramps off to Florida—and you did it the minute they retired—why, they would never ever die. (Or at least you wouldn't find out about it till just before the reading of the will.) And the best part was, since they were way down in Florida, they couldn't nag you about not visiting them. Ha!

Sociology also gave us something else—the snap college course. Now students could spend a whole year without ever lifting a book. College life became PARTY TIME, ALL THE TIME!

It therefore became necessary to invent the Spring Break to keep students from getting bored from partying in the same place, day in and day out. These two factors caused the population of Florida to zoom to over three zillion—in the winter. On May 1st, it goes back to seven.

There are no middle-aged people in Florida; they all live in the Midwest. (Except for Dick Clark, who actually died twenty-five years ago, but you wouldn't know it because his picture is permanently painted on your television screen.) So the three zillion people are equally divided: half are younger than anyone has a right to be and the other half are older than any of them want to be. And all of them are on drugs. Especially the snow birds, who have prescribing doctors in both places.

The young have their illegal drugs, and the old have their prescription drugs, so the roads are filled with infantile Al Unsers handling their vehicles like unguided missiles, and complacent Grandma Moseses handling theirs like tricycles, all of them oblivious to the fact that Detroit made more than just the one car they're driving.

The Florida State Legislature is doing its best to keep the population down. They have outlawed turn signals and sidewalks, and imported Panamanian cockroaches with the size and viciousness of Noriega's fighting roosters. Who, because of his great love for the U.S., provides them free.

The state is divided into two parts: Disney World and Not Disney World. The people who go to Disney World are never told the rest of the state exists. The NDW part of the state is further divided into three parts: East Coast, West Coast and Miami. Actually there is a middle too, but nobody ever uses it—the only reason they have it is to keep the three main parts apart.

In Miami, you'll find a drug store on every corner, whether there's a storefront or not. The three most-used words there are *cash, cocaine,* and *andale.*

The old people spend their days filling sacks with seashells, and their nights creating early-bird waiting lines in restaurants.

The young spend their days drinking six-packs on the beach and their nights playing Splat—an elimination game of jumping from twentieth-floor balconies.

Both young and old play the car-rental game, wherein you try to guess how much that $10-a-day chariot is really going to cost you. I usually base my estimates on last year's charges, plus maybe 10%. But my estimates are always too low because they keep inventing new charges. There's the airport fee, extra driver fee, and a $12.99 gas fee for a car that won't take eight bucks' worth if the needle is kicking E in the ass. (Don't forget this article was originally written in the early 70's.) And a daily insurance fee that would, if figured as an annual rate, generate enough money to buy the Sears building in less than three years. My $49 per week car only cost me $266.03 for ten days.

When your vacation is all over, you pick up your luggage from the airline's luggage lottery people—who have usually found it from your incoming trip just in time for your flight home.

15. 'Tis Fall (when a young man's fancy turns lightly to thoughts of leaves)

Well, it does if he has a yard to look after. And here on Muck Lake, Starr and I are blessed with one large enough to graze both cattle and sheep with nary a hint of range war.

Let me start by stating that I fudged a little there. The real name of our lake is Crystal Lake. "Crystal" is a right and proper name for it, too, because it's as clear as can be—except in the deepest parts, of course. This clearness is both a blessing and a curse. You can see the bottom, and all the beautiful marine flora and fauna but you can also see a shitload of bottles, cans and discarded tops of plastic worm containers.

And that my friends, is Crystal Lake—a prism of purity, a continuum of clarity, as blessed a body as ever viewed by humans—that is, until you step into it. One footfall raises enough muck to—well, that's not entirely correct; you can't possibly consider each footfall a step, when your feet keep sinking until you thank God for inventing crotches.

Whence cometh this muck? Thousands of years of accumulated desiccating, deciduous detritus. The same stuff you rake annually from your lawn into a pile, later claiming to have no knowledge of who started it on fire, and gee, Officer, I guess it must have been some kids. Besides, who cares? Everyone loves the smell of burning leaves, and I'll bet the cop burns his too, even though there's an ordinance against it. And don't tell me with that goody-goody two-shoes air that you don't, because even if you don't, I've seen you shoveling snow out into the road on warm winter days so that cars would turn it into slush and get rid of it for you. And here's a news flash: that's also illegal, so, there!

In Syracuse (New York, not Italy), you must rake the leaves into the street for the street sweeper to pick up. You may not put them in bags. One year, I bagged them, and the city made me dump them all out. They were later picked up and redistributed on my lawn by Mariah, a nor'wester quite aptly named by the storm-naming people. Boy, was I pissed!

In the City of Jackson, (near where we live in Michigan), you must bag your leaves and take them on specified dates to specified drop sites where they charge you a specified amount per specified bag size. Last year a buddy of mine missed the specified date, so we loaded his collection into the back of Big Whitey (my truck) and toted it to my house in the country where it is not illegal to burn it. It took three days to feed it to my burn barrel.

Unfortunately, when it came to my own leaves, the crop was so huge that it was impractical to burn it, unless I either had a month to spare or wanted my yard to look like Atlanta after Sherman's little visit. So I loaded it all into Big Whitey and took it to a private dump site, which was actually just a big crater. It took about four truck loads to haul it all.

After I had backed the truck up to the ravine and dumped the last load, I realized that my contributions had filled the pit to a depth of lotsa very deep—maybe even six feet. The tailgate of the truck was only about four feet above the leaves.

I looked around and did not see a soul. I was alone on a sunny day, standing next to what had to be the most humongous pile of autumn leaves I would ever see in my life.

"Ah, what the heck!"

The Indian arrow took me square in the chest; I turned with a groan, and dying, tumbled from the back of my Palomino into the box canyon below.

It was everything I remembered, and more. The thrill of letting go, of deliberately falling; the oh-so-soft, oh-so-slow landing that went on and on, as the crinkling, crunching leaves compressed below me. And the scent they released in a heavenly cloud all around me—oh, it was the smell of childhood, I'm telling you! It was the most freeing moment I'd had in years.

I'm pretty sure no one saw me. But if they did, I hope that

after I left, they did the same dang thang—because there are so few opportunities in life to feel the thrill of childhood again.

And because it's never too late to turn over a new leaf...or a whole pile of them.

Arturo's

"Decent" Italian Food

WELCOME!

Don't let our frivolous manner fool you into thinking that we're not serious about quality and service. We are.

HAVE YOUR NEXT AFFAIR WITH ME!

We cater parties, picnics, clambakes, office luncheons, orgies, etc

APPETIZERS & SIDES
Best on the Block

Steamed mussels..................................CHEAP
Steamed white clams............................DEAR

SUBS & SANGWIDGES
Best in the Neighborhood

Count Dracula – For those who go bats for round ~~stakes~~ steaks. Savory meatballs wallowing in sauce, topped with melted provolone You'll enjoy sinking your fangs in this one

Not a Babe on the Links – The tastiest Italian sausage in town, made by two Jewish boys, no less

Liberace's Love – Alias the half 'n' half. One sausage, two meatballs

Dino's Delight – Always better when sauced. Thin sliced steak, mixed with fried onions and garnished with Spaghetti Sauce

Let Menachem Go Beggin' – He may never know the joy of capicola ham with melted cheese, baked tomato and pepper wedges

Please order subs by number – just to drive the staff crazy

DINNERS
Best in The City

Baked Fake Ziti – Pasta shells, sauce, cheeses. One shell of a dish

Chicken Twigi – A flattened, breaded breast, served ala Parmesan

Yankee Noodle Dandy – Shells with EXTRA sharp cheese. Not for kids, you can take them home later and give them Chef Boy Ardee

Squishy Zuke – ~~Exactly something~~ nothing like eggplant Parmesan

Sloppy Lasagna – So much glop, it can't stand up on the plate

Deliberator's Delight – Sides of lasagna, zuke parm, balls, shrooms, and a link. Bring a wheelbarrow and a friend to get you home

Monk's Roast – Baked monkfish. I wanted to have a Friars Roast, but it's too hard to keep them in the pan

Shrimp Scampi Prawn Crustacea – Over redundant? No! No! No!

Bad Breath Bonanza – Clams, mussels, shrimp over Spaghetti with garlic butter sauce, An odor that can't be refused

Little Egypt – Surf & Turf. Not just a strip, but a piece o' tail, too

JUST DESSERTS
Best in the State
Chocolate Amaretto Pie / Strawberry Cheese Cake

PIZZA
Best in the World

Specialty Pies – King's Prawn, Mean Greens, Meatsa Pizza, White Knight, Bad Breath, Naked

Extras – The usual stuff plus Capicola, Salami, Olives, Tiny Shrimp, Grated Cheese, Tomato wedges, Meatball, Pepperoncini, Broccoli

Sorry, the sauerkraut and whip cream pizza has been discontinued

BEVERAGES
Not Any Better than Anyone Else's

Made in the USA
San Bernardino, CA
10 October 2014